JESUS · THE · IMAGINATION

French Postcard, unattributed

JESUS · THE · IMAGINATION

A JOURNAL OF
SPIRITUAL REVOLUTION

The Garden

VOLUME FOUR
2020

Angelico Press

Published by
ANGELICO PRESS

Edited by
Michael Martin

Typesetting & Design by
James R. Wetmore

Send inquiries to:
Editorial Office
The Center for Sophiological Studies
Stella Matutina Farm
8780 Moeckel Road
Grass Lake, MI 49240
USA
mmartin@jesustheimagination.com
734-445-7327

ISBN 978-1-62138-554-7 pb

Front Cover: Cheri Davis
Angel, Adare Augustinian Friary

Back Cover: Cheri Davis
Garden at St. Finbar's Oratory

Cover Design: Michael Schrauzer

CONTENTS

frontis-   FRENCH POSTCARD
piece

1   INTRODUCTION: THE GARDEN
     by Michael Martin

3   NOSTALGIA FOR THE ALKAHEST *by* Isak Bond

4   COMING TO EARTH *by* Jeremy Naydler

25   EVE, ONE AFTERNOON *by* Philippa Martyr

26   THE SEASIDE CEMETERY *by* Paul Valéry

32   GARDEN GATE *by* Therese Schroeder-Sheker

49   PENANT MELANGELL *by* Jon Egan

50   SAINT JOHN OF THE WILDERNESS *by* Tyler DeLong

51   CHERRY SAPLINGS *by* Ruth Asch

52   A PLACE TO LIVE *by* Jonathan Monroe Geltner

56   IN THE KINGDOM OF THE QUEEN:
     An Interview with Gunther Hauk, with Michael Martin

63   PEACEFUL WATERS *by* Katie Hartsock

65   THE TREES ARE BENDING THEIR NECKS
     by John R. P. Russell

66   THE GARDEN OF WISDOM *by* Andrew Kuiper

77 FOUR POEMS *by* R. Bratten Weiss

81 TWO POEMS *by* Rick Yoder

82 BERRY PICKING *by* Paul Hunter

83 THE WORLD AS GARDEN *by* Scot F. Martin

86 MATINS *by* Tom Sturch

91 GARDENS: SITES OF RESISTANCE *by* Darrell Lackey

97 THE WAR AGAINST SLOTH: PAUL TYSON,
    MOSHE IDEL, AND THE SLEEPWALKERS
    by Michael Martin

103 THE SIGNATURE OF ALL THINGS *by* Kenneth Rexroth

106 CONTRIBUTORS

Introduction:
The Garden

Michael Martin
Stella Matutina Farm
The Center for Sophiological Studies

HAT IS IT ABOUT GAR-dens that so fascinates us? Certainly, cultivation of a natural space transforms, transfigures that space into something not quite "natural" and not quite artificial—a space marked by the participation of the human with the environment that changes both. But as Jeremy Naydler points out in these pages, a tension between creative interaction and the desire for complete domination also colors this relationship. But there is also in this garden, this between place, this metaxu, the possibility of divine participation. Eden is a garden, not a forest.

The awareness of the sacred connected with the cultivation of nature is not something particular to the Judeo-Christian traditions. Japanese gardens, for example, also open the human being into a dimension of the sacred, a feeling that is palpable for anyone who has visited one. In Classical Rome, Virgil sensuously illuminated the phenomena of grace made possible by cultivation:

Above all, worship the gods, and pay great Ceres her yearly rites, sacrificing on the glad sward, with the setting of winter's last days, when clear springtime has now come. Then are lambs fat and wine is most mellow; then sweet is sleep, and thick are the shadows on the hills. Then let all your country folk worship Ceres; for her wash the honeycomb with milk and soft wine, and three times let the luck-bearing victim pass round the young crops, while the whole choir of your comrades follow exulting, and loudly call Ceres into their homes; nor let any put his sickle to the ripe corn, ere for Ceres he crown his brows with oaken wreath, dance artless measures, and chant her hymns.[1]

The sense of the sacred union of the agricultural cycle, that is to say "gardening," with the sacred calendar is more and more lost to us, though not completely obliterated. At my farm, for example, we strive to connect the growing season to the Church calendar (generally ignored by the Church, alas). May Day, St. John's, and Michaelmas are enormously important to our farm and our community of friends who join us in these celebrations. The seventeenth-century

---

[1] *Georgics* 1. 336–50 in Virgil, *Eclogues, Georgics, Aeneid I–VI*, trans. H. Rushton Fair-clough, Loeb Classic Library (Harvard University Press, 1922).

Anglican priest and poet Robert Herrick celebrated these as well, for he reveled in the pagan, the Christian, and the folk traditions of his time in his poetry—traditions that were under attack by the Puritan killjoys then in power. We have our own killjoys today. Don't let them win.

Of course, the coldness of our times notwithstanding, the garden is not always edenic. We contend with weather—like the frost in late May this year, flooding, drought—not to mention insect damage and the unintended destruction wrought by deer. In addition, industrial agriculture has poisoned the environment and inflicted illness on untold millions. And I don't even need to mention Gethsemane.

In the classic children's book *The Secret Garden* by Frances Hodgson Burnett we encounter the young protagonist, Mary Lennox, whose parents both died in India and who is sent to live with her uncle, a man incapacitated by the death of his wife, and her cousin, made invalid by a dreadful combination of emotional neglect and "modern" scientific treatments. The gardens around the manor likewise suffer from atrophy and neglect. The book depicts a psychic and literal wasteland caused by trying to escape life, even the uncomfortable parts of life—like death. After she meets the intrepid Yorkshire boy Dickon, a friend to animals and who knows the names of all the flowers, Mary approaches her uncle, Mr. Craven, with a request:

"Might I," quavered Mary, "might I have a bit of earth?"
In her eagerness she did not realize how queer the words would sound and that they were not the ones she had meant to say. Mr. Craven looked quite startled.

"Earth!" he repeated. "What do you mean?"

"To plant seeds in—to make things grow—to see them come alive," Mary faltered.[2]

Craven, whose deceased wife had loved the gardens, finds himself moved, ever so slightly, away from the morose grip of death at the child's request.

"You can have as much earth as you want," he said. "You remind me of someone else who loved the earth and things that grow. When you see a bit of earth you want," with something like a smile, "take it, child, and make it come alive."

As I look at the world in this strangest of years, I am reminded that what we lack is a relationship to the Real. By "the Real" I mean *the Life that participates in and, occasionally, shines through all life*. If you really want to change the world, maybe the best place to start is with a packet of seeds.

Stella Matutina Farm
7 June 2020

---

[2] Frances Hodgson Burnett, *The Secret Garden*, ed. Gretchen Holbrook Gerzina, Norton Critical Editions (Norton, 2006), 70.

NOSTALGIA FOR THE ALKAHEST

Isak Bond

"…*young Master Shemmy on his very first debouch at the very dawn of protohistory seeing himself such and such, when playing with thistlewords in their garden nursery*…"

JAMES JOYCE, *Finnegans Wake*

I planted seeds this spring,
each a struck match
flaring in the night-black earth,

points of warmth,
hot little future buds embedded
within, waiting

for the soil's embrace,
the kisses of the rain,
what will be streamed

in the grain, a wager
in the shadow of winter, a bet
on a great upcoming

bonfire of petals blooming.
But still, the air whispers
that I liked the lighting

of it best, the earth
giving way beneath my boots,
the happy scattering.

With the flowers on their way,
I miss the flame original.
A beginning begun

is done.

Coming to Earth

Jeremy Naydler

The Hercules Complex

Amongst the many different exploits of Hercules, who is one of the great hero-figures of Western mythology, was a wrestling match with a little known giant called Antaeus. Whereas Hercules was the son of a mortal woman, Antaeus was the son of the earth goddess Gaia. Antaeus lived in a cave and slept on the earth, and drew all his strength from being constantly in contact with the earth. Antaeus could be understood from an archetypal perspective as representing the primal human being.

In this red figure vase from the 6th century BC, we see the two wrestling. Hercules is on the left, Antaeus is on the right. Behind Hercules is Athena, his warrior goddess mentor. Behind Antaeus is his mother Gaia, but she is really *underneath* him, because she is the earth.

In the wresting match, Hercules repeatedly throws Antaeus to the ground, but each time Antaeus rises up with renewed strength, because he draws all his strength from the earth.

Figure 1: *Hercules and Antaeus wrestling. Red figure vase, 6th c. BC. Louvre Museum, Paris*

And Antaeus would have defeated Hercules had not Hercules realized what was happening. Hercules realises that the only way to defeat Antaeus is to lift him above the ground in a great bear hug, and to hold him in the air so his feet are off the earth. Unable to touch the earth, Antaeus is no match against Hercules, who slowly squeezes him to death. And all the while Antaeus's mother Gaia wails and groans beneath him.

This gruesome story has a direct bearing on our situation today, for these two figures continue to contend within our souls. Their wrestling match is not yet done, for there is an Antaeus in all of us, struggling to free himself from the deathlike grip of Hercules. Let us look more closely at Hercules, and what he has come to represent in our collective mythology.

In Roman times and then later in the Renaissance, Hercules was regarded as one of the main archetypal figures to be invoked in the effort to subjugate the forces of nature. In the Renaissance, he became the patron of great engineering projects. And in the grand Renais-

Roman model, can be seen in the garden of the chateau of Vaux-le-Vicomte in France. Vaux is about thirty miles south of Paris, and the garden was the work of Le Nôtre, who was employed by Louis XIV's finance minister (who owned the chateau) to produce something really impressive. The garden required the destruction of three villages, the diversion of a river and the employment of eighteen thousand labourers. After levelling the ground, a series of promenades, parterres, pools with fountains, canals and water cascades were all laid out.[1] It was a triumphant imposition of human ratio-

Figure 2: *Statue of Hercules at Vaux-le-Vicomte*

sance gardens, which tended to be the product of massive engineering works, statues of Hercules would often be erected. An example of one such statue, based on an earlier

nality, order and engineering prowess on the natural landscape. Hercules's

[1] Ronald King, *The Quest for Paradise* (Weybridge: Whittet Books, 1979), 155.

antagonism towards nature was not limited to his wrestling match with the son of Gaia. Many, if not

to the human will. The question is: How can we break free of its suffocating grip?

Figure 3: *Hercules Ension XX638 Wheel Loader/mini excavator*

most, of the "Labors of Hercules" were about using brute force to dominate nature—capturing the fiery Cretan bull, mastering the savage Thracian mares, subduing the fierce Erymanthian boar, killing the raging Nemean lion—so how appropriate that in the Renaissance he ruthlessly imposes his will on whole landscapes. Of all the ancient Greek heroes, he is the one who asserts human power over nature.

It is therefore no surprise to see him incarnate in modern times as a ten and a half ton excavator, such as the one in Figure 3. He's at home with technologies dedicated to the dominance and control of the earth. But my point is that today one can't help but feel we are all in the grip of the "the Hercules complex," which could be defined as the imperative to subjugate nature—and all that is natural—

Adam "From the Soil"

There is a beautiful twelfth-century mosaic in the cathedral of Monreale, near Palermo, in Sicily. It depicts the creation of Adam by God after the plants and animals have been created. Adam is shown emerging from—or rising up out of—a mound of earth. Above him are plant forms and animals.

It is always salutary to remember that we are called human beings because we are made of the earth. Adam literally means "from the soil" and our word "human" etymologically shares the same root as "humus."[2] In the Book of Genesis, God made Adam out of the earth. It is usually translated as "dust" but

---

[2] For Adam (*adamah*), meaning "from the soil," see Bernhard W. Anderson, *The Living World of the Old Testament* (Harlow: Long-

the meaning is not so much "dry dust"as the fertile topsoil or humus.[3]

It is not just the Judaeo-Christian tradition that tells us we are made of earth. Practically every other ancient and traditional culture had a similar idea. In ancient Greek mythology, according to one account, the first human beings were moulded from the earth by Prometheus, but the earliest myths tell of how humans sprang directly from the earth mother Gaia.[4] This is why Antaeus represents the primal human being. There are similar accounts in traditional cultures all over the world. For example, Native American myths also tell of the first humans emerging directly from the earth mother.[5]

At the cathedral of Monreale, there is another mosaic (Fig. 5) which depicts God introducing Eve to Adam, who now sits comfortably on his mound of earth while God and Eve walk towards him. For some time I could not understand why I felt unusually moved by this picture, but then I rea-

Figure 4: *The Creation of Adam. 12th-century mosaic, Monreale Cathedral, Sicily*

man, 1978), 212. For the etymology of "humus" see Ernest Klein, *A Comprehensive Etymological Dictionary of the English Language* (London: Emerald Group Publishing, 2008), 355.

[3] For the Hebrew word *afar,* usually translated as "dust," see Carl Friedrich Keil and Franz Delitzsch, *Commentary on the Old Testament,* vol.1 (Peabody, MA: Hendrickson Publishers, 1996), Gen. 2.7. Also Joel M. Hoffman, *The Bible Doesn't Say That: 40 Biblical Mistranslations* (New York: St. Martin's Press, 2016), 102–4.

[4] Carl Kerenyi, *The Gods of the Greeks* (Harmondsworth: Penguin, 1958), 184–89.

[5] Guy Cooper, "The Origins of Humanity," in Roy Willis, ed., *World Mythology* (London: BCA, 1993), 223.

lized that it is because it shows not only Adam, Eve and God but also an essential yet easily missed fourth presence: the humble earth on which all of them depend. From the very beginning of our existence, the earth has supported us, standing, walking, sitting and lying down.

One of the wonders of human existence is that the earth is solid underneath us. We know it won't give way, we won't sink into it as we sink into the sea, and we won't fall through it as we fall through the air. We are able to live our lives in the confidence that the earth will support our weight. If we were to ask ourselves the simple question, "what do we really feel towards the earth?" surely one feeling we should all have would be *a sense of gratitude* for its reliability. Imagine how difficult life would be if we could never be sure that the earth beneath our feet would hold us up, and that at any moment it might give way and we might sink into it. We shouldn't take these things for granted.

Figure 5: *God introduces Eve to Adam. 12th-century mosaic, Monreale Cathedral, Sicily*

The poem that follows expresses this sense of gratitude for the miraculous fact that each day we are able to walk upon the firm earth, and live our lives as children of the earth, trusting in her benevolence.

DEAR EARTH

Dear Earth, on you we stand,
we neither float nor sink.
You bear the weight
of every living thought we think.
We thank you that you keep
so firm and meek beneath
our wandering wingless feet.

Though we may spurn you,
bruise, abuse and disown you,
the flight of our desire
must come to land, come home,
come down, to you
our deepest bond,
upon the ground,
that we by obligation bound,
might till and tend
and make amend
to you, our friend.

Just as the Native American creation myths speak of humanity emerging from the earth, so the sense of connectedness to the earth runs through Native American spirituality as its sacred core. There was no hero-figure like Hercules, whose *raison d'être* was to subdue nature. The Native Americans kept the primal, sacred bond with the earth. Figure 6 shows an old photograph of Chief Luther Standing Bear, who was born in the 1860s, a terrible time to be born as a so-called "Indian." He saw the destruction of his people and he made it his life's purpose to try to articulate and preserve the traditional Native American view of the world.

He tells us that the Lakota tribe never sat propped up in chairs like the white people because they "came literally to love the soil and they sat or reclined on the ground with a feeling of being close to a mothering power…. The soil was soothing, strengthening, cleansing and healing."[6] He describes how the Lakota always went back to the soil, to the earth, to regain their energy: they always

Figure 6: *Chief Luther Standing Bear*

[6] Luther Standing Bear, *Land of the Spotted Eagle* (Lincoln and London: University of Nebraska Press, 1978), 192.

felt better for being in contact with the earth. And then he says: "the Lakota knew that the human heart, away from nature, becomes hard… knew that lack of respect for growing, living things soon led to lack of respect for humans too."[7]

The Lakota understood that the connection with the earth keeps the human heart soft, empathetic, and open. Why? Because the human heart is nourished by the earth and by all the creatures of the earth. That is why people away from nature become hard-hearted. The earth brings us back to our own souls, to the inner psychic ground on which we humanly must stand. And this inner ground is what gives us empathy for all other earth-born creatures. Without this feeling for other creatures, we soon lose respect for other human beings.

we spend asleep.[8] We are rapidly becoming adjusted to living our lives through electronic media, and as the balance shifts away from direct contact with nature and with other human beings, the words of Chief Luther Standing Bear are increasingly relevant. While of course we need to adjust our lifestyles to keep abreast of the times, the danger is that in so doing we lose touch with our own souls, with what is essential to being human.

Figure 7: *The great migration from the real to the virtual world*

The Great Migration

Today we are living through one of the greatest migrations of human beings ever, the migration from the real world to the virtual world (Fig. 7). According to a recent UK survey, the amount of time spent by adults on media and communications, which includes TV, radio, cinema, telephone, mobile phone, internet accessed through PC, laptop, tablet, and smartphone, etc. is now just under nine hours per day, roughly half of our waking hours, and more than the time

Roughly eighty years ago, in the late 1920s, E. M. Forster wrote a novella called *The Machine Stops*, in which he describes how human beings in the future conduct all their communication with each other through videolink: no one talks directly to anyone else, no one directly sees anyone else, no one touches anyone else. All communication is electronically mediated, and this is regarded as a mark of civilization. In this civilization of the future, human beings no longer live in

[7] Ibid., 197.

[8] Ofcom *Communications Market Report*: 4th August, 2016, 5.

nature, but have built vast cities underground, where everyone lives in separate cells. It is as if humanity has

Figure 8: *The new norm of social communication*

fallen below the level of nature into the subnatural world. And there, deep under the earth, they live in the belly of a vast global electric machine. The machine has subsumed them and they have become so used to the background hum of the machine that no one even notices it. No one has time to reflect on their situation because all are continually distracted by trivial pursuits conducted entirely through the omnipresent machine with which they constantly interact and upon which they have come to depend.

The photograph reproduced in Figure 8 portrays a new norm of social communication. The Ofcom survey that I just referred to states that half of the teenagers interviewed had communicated with someone via their digital device while in the same room as the other person.[9] Perhaps

those shown in Figure 8 are in fact all texting or tweeting each other, but would that make it better or worse than if they were communicating with people elsewhere? We daily witness how we are moving closer and closer to the world that E. M. Forster's *The Machine Stops* describes.

Three years ago the Natural History Museum in London proudly launched its new "Virtual Reality Experience" in collaboration with Samsung, so visitors to the museum could experience "total immersion" in audio-visual content. The photograph of the VIPs invited to the launch

Figure 9: *"Discovering the natural world like never before"*

shows them experiencing "total immersion" (Fig. 9). Referring to the occasion, the president of Samsung Electronics UK said, "We are delighted to be working with the Natural History Museum on this project, helping people to discover the natural world like never before."[10]

The irony of this seemed to be lost on all the participants, including Sir David Attenborough, who can be seen sitting in the middle—it was one of his nature films they were all watching, of course!

We have to ask ourselves: is this really the way forward? If we have become such strangers to the natural world that we have to *discover* it, like some hitherto unknown planet, then

The Fantasy of Abandoning the Earth

In a publicity brochure recently put out by Space X, the company owned by billionaire Elon Musk, we are asked to embrace the idea that we should think of ourselves as a multi-planetary species. One of the reasons for this is that Elon Musk believes that the earth will eventually become uninhabitable, so he wants to set up a colony on Mars.[11]

It is interesting that the lure of virtual reality coincides with the fantasy

Figure 10: *Lifting off from the earth. From Space X publicity brochure, "Making Life Multiplanetary" (2017)*

are VR headsets really going to help us? Would it not be better to go for a walk with our senses alert and our minds curious? When did we last stop to really look at a wildflower? How many wildflowers do we know by name? How many different trees can we identify? When did we last look at the stars? Do we know what phase the moon is in?

of becoming a multi-planetary species. Both involve surrendering to the temptation to abandon the Earth, and both are symptomatic of a profound lack of any real sense of connectedness with nature. With this lack of feeling for nature goes a lack of consciousness of our responsibility for the fate of the Earth.

A few months before he died, Stephen Hawking backed up Musk's

---

[10] Natural History Museum press release, 5 June 2015.

[11] Elon Musk, "Making Humans a Multi-Planetary Species" in *New Space*, 5.2 (June 2017), 46.

dismal prognosis of the Earth's future. Hawking said that we must start leaving our planet *within thirty years* to avoid being wiped out by over-population and climate change. He argued that the only viable solution to our current problems is to establish colonies on the Moon and Mars. Hawking proposed that we should take "a Noah's Ark of plants, animals, fungi and insects to start creating a new world."[12]

It seems we are to imagine filling space rockets with cows and sheep, chickens and goats, grasses and trees, mushrooms and bees, which will somehow be looked after while they

on a planet that has an atmosphere composed of 96% carbon dioxide and with roughly one third less gravity than we experience here on Earth. It would be like going to live in a very cold desert (temperatures have been recorded as low as minus 140 degrees centigrade) but with no breathable air. Elon Musk absurdly suggests that the lack of gravity would provide the opportunity to "have fun" and "bound around."[13] I suspect that those who weren't too cold to think or feel anything would swiftly tire of their relative weightlessness and long once more to feel their weight upon the ground beneath them.

Figure 11: *The colony on Mars, envisaged by Space X,*
"Making Life Multiplanetary" (2017)

speed away from the Earth, weightlessly floating around the rocket, on a trip lasting a minimum of eighty days. It would surely be complete pandemonium! And once Noah's Ark finally landed, and the animals and humans disembarked, they would be arriving

The grand plan is that the plants transported to Mars from Earth would convert the CO_2 into oxygen. But we are talking here of a whole planet's atmosphere lacking a vital life-sustaining ingredient—oxygen! How many plants over how many thousands of years are going to be needed to convert the atmosphere of

---

[12] Sarah Knapton, "Human race is doomed if we do not colonize Moon and Mars, says Stephen Hawking," *The Telegraph*, 20 June 2017.

[13] Elon Musk, op. cit., 46.

Mars into a life-supporting environment? And, of course, plants need decent soil to grow in. Meanwhile, what are the sheep, cows and goats going to feed on, let alone breathe? Not only will they need eighty days' supply of food for the trip (which would surely require a large barn to be attached to the rocket), but once they have landed they will be in a freezing cold, airless desert with nothing whatsoever to eat. One can't help but think that it would be a lot easier to concentrate on bringing fertility back to the deserts and desolated soils of our own planet by (for a start) planting trees here on Earth to reclaim the deserts and replace the catastrophic destruction of the Earth's forests! That would at least address one of the reasons (climate change) for abandoning the Earth in the first place.

Despite the impracticality of the Martian project, many people have got extremely excited about leaving the Earth to its doom and becoming a multi-planetary species, including other billionaire business men, like Richard Branson of Virgin fame, and Jeff Bezos, the founder of Amazon. The media celebrity scientist Brian Cox is also an enthusiast, eagerly looking forward to our becoming "a space-faring civilization."[14] If you do not find yourself swept up in all the boyish excitement, the likelihood is that you, like me, feel dumbfounded at the arrogance, the reckless irresponsibility and the sheer profligacy of these men, who seem to care so little for the planet they actually live on.

[14] Brian Cox, "Why Mars is first for human colonization and then beyond," in *National Geographic,* 26 March 2018.

Becoming Cyborg

There is a curious paradox, which accompanies the fantasy of leaving the planet, and perhaps could be understood as the shadow cast upon us by the flight of the imagination away from the Earth. Just as this flight upwards is carried on the wings of dizzying fantasy, so it is matched by advances in technology that seem to bind us ever more closely to machines. One of these advances is in the field of "Brain to Computer Interface" (BCI) technologies. As they grow ever more sophisticated, they offer the prospect of instant communication with, and control over, our digital devices without the intervention of any tangible medium. Gone is the need for the traditional mouse and keyboard: computers and robots can now be controlled by thought alone. And so BCI technologies also promise to integrate our inner life more and more seamlessly with machines. What is being held out to us is not simply a one-way "command and control" functionality, but rather a new kind of intimacy between the computer and the human psyche.

Figure 12 shows a man wearing an Electro-encephalogram (EEG) net over his head. The net monitors electrical signals in the brain, which can be converted into digital signals, enabling the person to operate a computer or smartphone or any other digital device through thought control. In order to achieve this kind of thought control, the human being is enmeshed in an electronic mantle that effectively binds him to the machine.

In Figure 13 below, we see a woman wearing an EEG net facing a robot.

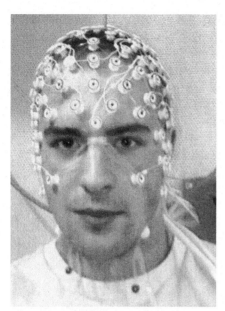

Figure 12: *EEG Recording Net, that binds the human being to the machine*

The woman and the machine stare at each other across a table, and the caption tells us that her brain waves are classified in milliseconds by the computer, to which her brain is linked, she has to surrender a considerable degree of autonomy to the computer. As much as we see the machine as an extension of the human being, we also see the human being becoming an extension of the machine. Thus the more we seek to integrate our lives with machines, the more they seem to present themselves as mirror images of ourselves.

Already we can observe this happening in the widespread re-conception of human nature in the image of the machine. This began in the eighteenth century with La Mettrie's groundbreaking book, *L'homme machine* ("Man a Machine") in which he compared the workings of the brain to clockwork. Today, many people seriously believe that our brains are nothing more than "biological computers" or "biochemical algorithms."[15] While the technology can be adapted to try

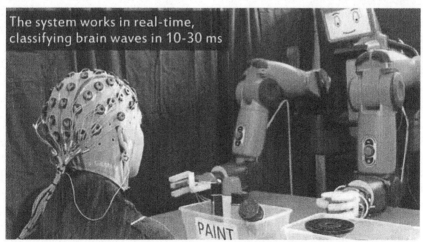

The system works in real-time, classifying brain waves in 10-30 ms

Figure 13: *Facing a reduced version of ourselves. From CSAIL, MIT, "Mind Control: Correcting robot mistakes using EEG brain signals"*

puter that is monitoring her, enabling more or less instantaneous communication with the robot. Because she can only control the robot via a sophisti-

[15] Richard Dawkins, *The God Delusion* (London: Random House, 2007), 412; Yuval Noah Harari, *Homo Deus* (London: Vintage, 2015), 328ff.

to make it look cool and stylish (as in Figure 14 below), the underlying tendency is very clear: the human being, reconceived in the image of the machine, becomes a kind of adjunct to it. The more we integrate the human mind with machines, the more the human being is drawn away from the human into the orbit of the inhuman. In this way humanity falls under the shadow of the machine, while all the time thinking that we are extending our control over it.

through wood three inches thick. But the reality is that the more he becomes a mechanical Hercules, the more his humanity is squeezed out by Hercules's iron grip. What is human in him has not been enhanced, but subsumed, by the exoskeleton. The soldier has metamorphosed into a machine-human hybrid, a cyborg.

As well as superhuman strength, the new technologies also promise superhuman *intelligence*, as Artificial Intelligence continues to develop

Figure 14: *Man wearing an Emotiv EPOC Headset controls robot arm*

In recent years the development of the exoskeleton has taken this tendency to a bizarre extreme, in which the human being is all but lost to view. In Figure 15 an American soldier does press-ups, wearing an exoskeleton, which gives him phenomenal extra strength. The idea is that the soldier is made into a super-strong Hercules, capable of amazing physical feats. He can lift weights far beyond normal human capacity and can punch

extremely rapidly and brain-machine interfaces become increasingly sophisticated. We are living at a time when the image of the human being as a machine-human has taken root in the collective consciousness. Many popular thinkers, for example Ray Kurzweil, Stephen Hawking, Yuval Noah Harari, and others, seriously believe that the future of humanity is to transcend our biology by becoming fully integrated with machines. Many also believe that our technologies can eventually even "defeat death" (the twelfth labour of Hercules). Some years ago, Google launched a company dedicated to solving "the problem" of aging and to actively exploring the possibility of endless life-extension on the physical plane.[16] Thereby might we become as gods, transforming from mere *Homo Sapiens* to *Homo Deus*, the "God Man." The following poem gives voice to the terrifying delusion, with its attendant ambitions.

[16] Harry McCracken and Lev Grossman, "Google vs. Death," *Time Magazine*, 30 September 2013.

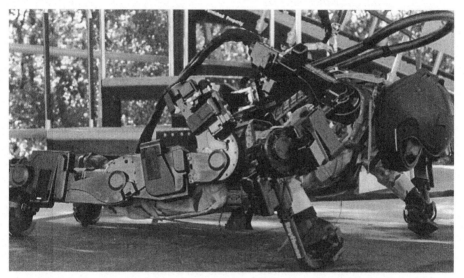

Figure 15: *A soldier, wearing an endoskeleton, does press-ups. ZDNet, September 29, 2010*

HOMO DEUS

How great shall we become:
We shall drill the barren desert and frack the wilderness
we shall mine the proud mountain,
break the stubborn earth and bend it to our will,
we shall purge the life-infested soil with our chemicals
and every living thing that opposes us we shall destroy.

We shall eradicate the dandelion and dock,
wild poppy and pimpernel, nettle, cornflower,
cow parsley and cowering violet—
we shall vanquish them all,
so that our fields may be perfectly uniform:
and they shall harbour no pestilential insects
for we shall destroy the insects that devour our crops,

the insects that bite and those that sting,
destroy the ant, mosquito, wasp and bee,
hornet and horsefly, butterfly, beetle, moth and flea,
every ignoble, buzzing creature that God in his delusion
has made to stand against us.
And the birds of hedgerow and field,
of woodland and meadow, corn-bunting,
cuckoo and wren,
shall cease their singing.

We shall crush the viper, smoke out badger and fox;
the wild boar and wolf shall no more disturb our peace.
Our pigs shall be kept in soundproof facilities
under hygienic conditions,
and our cattle shall be raised in concrete barns
so that the world is made clean
and nothing is left save what is useful to us.

And we shall fill the world with machines
and equip them with integrated circuits and sensors,
to record, memorize, analyze and reason things out,
and every living creature shall be tagged and monitored
and the data shall be stored for future reference.

The world shall be made pure and electrical,
the air shall be filled with electromagnetic radiation
to make the planet smart,
and if the earth cry out, then none shall hear it,
for the people shall have earphones in their ears,
and shall be endlessly distracted by their screens,
so none shall notice the abomination of desolation.

Though some may sleep in Faraday cages
and paint their walls with zinc,
others shall know a new era
of order and distraction has dawned,
in which all obey the rules and follow the instructions,
and shall prefer puerile fantasy to living symbols,
for the brains of infants shall be cleansed,
and the angels shall be driven from the portals of light,
and the wisdom of the ancients
shall be cast into oblivion,
and the voice of conscience shall grow faint,

and none shall notice the desolation of imagination,
for the paths of thought shall be made straight,
and all shall tread the straight paths,
for by the straight paths shall we become great.

We shall mine the asteroids
we shall build cities on the Moon and Mars;
with our spaceships we shall storm the empyrean,
and we shall no longer be troubled by the Earth
with its potatoes and cabbages,
for we shall make ourselves clean and metallic,
and shall have no more need
of what is living and imperfect,
for we shall have become as gods.

Touching the Earth

We need to come back down to earth and to the reality of what it means to be human. To do this we must wake up from the intoxicating dream of technological omnipotence and free ourselves from the Hercules complex. It requires that we recover the experience of the wonder and mystery of being alive on planet Earth and belonging to the earth beneath our feet. It requires that we recognize that we are children of the earth.

The Buddha understood this. The sculpture depicted in Figure 16 shows the Buddha making the *Bhumisparsha* gesture—the gesture of "touching the earth." He made this gesture at the moment of his spiritual awakening. What led up to it was the most almighty struggle with the great adversary Mara, who did his best to throw him off course with fantasies, temptations and terrors. Through all of this the Buddha sat unmoved. And then Mara launched his deadliest attack, which was to whisper in the

Buddha's ear that everything he was doing was futile and pointless. Whatever he did on his own, sitting in a for-

Figure 16: *The Buddha makes the Bhumisparsha gesture of "touching the earth"*

est under a tree, had no significance either for the rest of the world or for humanity. Mara opened up the abyss of meaninglessness and despair and tried to get the Buddha to fall into it.

In response, the Buddha "touched the earth" with his right hand, calling the earth to be his witness that what he was doing was not just for himself but for all sentient beings. The gesture signified that he understood that if we fall out of relationship to the earth we become prey to our fantasies and delusions and forego our relationship to what is truly human.[17]

The question for us today is: How can we practice this gesture of "touching the earth" so we don't get carried away either by the fantasy of abandoning the Earth or the delusion that we can become godlike by remaking ourselves in the image of the machine?

[17] For the many versions of the temptation of the Buddha by Mara in both canonical and non-canonical texts, see Ananda W. P. Guruge, "The Buddha's Encounters with Mara the Tempter: Their Representation in Literature and Art," in *Sri Lanka Journal of Buddhist Studies,* 2 (1988).

How can we recover this gesture today? How can we bring the earth to bear witness to, and in a sense, *hold us to,* what is authentically human?

There are three things which I think we can do to practise this gesture. The first requires that we understand that to touch the earth is to touch the creatures that live on and within the earth. The gesture of touching the earth involves really caring for other creatures, especially the lowliest creatures that live in the soil—earwig and slug, woodlouse and worm. It has been estimated that since 1980, the population of invertebrates has declined by around 45%.[18] We have to understand that not only do these creatures depend on us, but we also depend on them. The humblest have their role to play. Here is a poem to the worm.

[18] Rodolfo Dirzo et al, "Defaunation in the Anthropocene," in *Science,* vol. 345, issue 6195 (2014), 401–6.

TO THE GENTLE WORM

Gentle worm within the soil
invisible to us you toil;
somewhere down beneath our feet
the earthy roots and grubs you greet.

Your form with mildness is imbued—
to other creatures you are food,
and yet none other would you harm
in anger, hunger, or alarm.

Your humble throat with earth you fill,
and from your mouth no sound does spill:
you do not growl, nor do you roar,
you do not have sharp tooth or claw,
nor fearsome horn nor poison fang.

When from the earth each creature sprang,
you stayed within your mother's womb,
unwilling to depart so soon,
swimming in the soil, your sea,
underneath the apple tree,
hidden from fierce angel's sight,
innocent of wrong and right.

And in your world where all is dark,
where no cat howls nor dog does bark,
hour on hour you toil away
and never know the light of day.

Do you ever laugh or weep?
Do you dream or fall asleep?
To whom is it your life belongs?
Your flesh feeds the blackbird's song,
and every thing that you excrete
nourishes the plants we eat.

The garden would, without you, die,
the blackbird lose its strength to fly,
the earth would sour and roots would rot,
deserts grow where you are not.

To you in gratitude we bend,
for on you do our lives depend.

While the Book of Genesis tells us that human beings are made from the soil, what it leaves out is the remarkable fact that human beings also have the capacity to *create* soil, to create humus. The creation of humus is the second way we can make the gesture of "touching the earth."

As well as the little creatures that live within the soil, today the soil itself is seriously afflicted. All over the world our soils are suffering degradation. Much of this is the result of intensive farming. In the UK alone we are losing over two million tons of fertile topsoil each year.[19] I don't know how many wheelbarrows that works out as, but all of us who have gardens, or allotments, or responsibility for any piece of land, no matter how small or large, can contribute to restoring the earth's fertility by making as much humus as we can and returning it to the soil.

Compost can be made in many different ways. Figure 18 shows one of my compost bins. It's made of strong plastic and has lasted many years, and it is one of the few uses of plastic that I am prepared to defend. It actually works remarkably well, and the bins are all teeming with life. We can think of the compost bin as being like an alchemical oven or athanor, combined with the alchemist's flask, in which amazing transmutations occur. In the old alchemical texts great importance was placed on maintaining a constant heat in order to ensure successful transmutation. Exactly the same thing is required for making good compost. Composting is a form of outdoor alchemy, each stage of which mirrors the transmutation of the soul. One of the most precious and profound things we can do as gardeners is to transmute base matter into the gold of really good compost. The following poem was written in homage to Keats' beautiful sonnet "Bright Star." It is called "Dark Heap."

[19] Intergovernmental Science-Policy Platform on Biodiversity and Ecosystem Services (IPBES) Report, March, 2018. For the UK, see FAO 1995/UN Millennium Ecosystem Assessment.

DARK HEAP

You are my athanor and flask,
the mirror of my inward task.
I die in you in shame and scorn,
I putrify, devoured by worm.

In you all my illusions burn;
in deep remorse to ash I turn:
from ash on ash and dust on dust
to love of life from life of lust.

Where leaf and stem from life are torn
there life again from death is born.

And richest soil is rotted dung –
such wealth from you, Dark Heap, is wrung:

by fools rejected and despised,
but it is treasured by the wise.

18: *The Dark Heap*

If the first thing we can do to practice the gesture of "touching the earth" is to look after vulnerable and lowly creatures, and the second thing we can do is to create humus, then the third thing we can do is to cultivate gratitude and praise, because gratitude and praise bring us back into connection with the wonder and mystery of our existence here on Earth.

Figure 19 shows a beautiful Roman mosaic of Orpheus, who during the 4th century was often identified with both King David, the praise-singing author of the psalms, and also with Christ. The figure represents the human being who is in harmony with the world of nature and the creatures of the earth. At the same time he is also in harmony with the heavenly world, whose energies he evokes with his seven-stringed (in this case double-stringed) lyre. So he takes his place between earth and heaven, which is where we all belong as human beings, fulfilling our human nature by caring for the earth and venerating the spiritual order represented by the heavens.[20] This doesn't mean that we live without difficulties and struggles, but it does mean that we can meet them with an attitude of thankfulness for the life that we have been given, and a reverence for the whole of creation.

[20] As is expressed in the Hermetic treatise, *Asclepius*, 8: "God made human beings out of the substance of spirit and the substance of body—out of that which is eternal and that which is mortal—blending together portions of each substance in the right measure, in order that the creature so fashioned might be able to fulfill the demands of both sources of its being: that is, to venerate and worship the things of heaven, and at the same time to tend and care for the things of earth."

Figure 19: *Orpheus, 4th-c. mosaic. RomanVilla at Phillippopolis, Shabda Museum, Syria*

PRAISE

I thank God for the silent stars that sing
above me, and for the earth beneath my feet,
for all the plants, dumb beasts and birds that bring
to this world such sweet innocence and peace.

I thank God too for the wasp that stings me,
and for the unremorseful snake that bites,
for the brambles on the path that scratch me,
and for the demon that against me fights.

I thank God for, thankless and unpraising,
we humans would our deepest purpose fail,
for self grows beyond itself through praising,
and prayer is like a breeze that fills our sail.

And so in gratitude I live my days,
giving to earth my love, to God my praise.

Illustration Sources

Wikimedia Commons: 1, 4, 5, 6; Bruno Denis (photo), 2; Brisbane Mini Excavators, 5; Source unknown, 7; Pinterest, 8, 19; Natural History Museum, London, 9; Space X, 10, 11; Organization for Human Brain Mapping, 12; Robohub.org, 13; Emotiv.com, 14; ZDNet, 15; Asia Society Museum, New York, 16; Jeremy Naydler, 17, 18.

EVE, ONE AFTERNOON

Philippa Martyr

Adamah my love
your brown skin warm and firm like a peeled nut
I watch you in the garden
your sweet slant eyes, seeds within a fruit
You are absorbed; you watch the leaves move
The beasts come nuzzling. You caress absently.
Your strong-stem fingers—
I know them; I know their strength in my shoulder,
around my waist
I know their tenderness; the underside of a flower
tracing the outline of my lips
Tangled entangled; the vine and the branches
You take my hands in yours; you place them on your chest
The liquid warmth beneath my fingers
So barely contained; so strong and yet so slender
Adamah my love

THE SEASIDE CEMETERY

Paul Valéry
(translated by *Jonathan Monroe Geltner*)

1.

This tranquil roof, where doves walk back and forth,
pulses between pines, among the tombstones.
There, noon, who is just, composes with fire
the sea—the sea always begun anew.
What compensation a lingering glance,
after thinking, upon the calm of gods.

2.

And what pure work, thin flashes of lightning,
consumes the diamonds of sightless seafoam,
what peace seems to be made and to quicken!
When a sun reposes on the abyss,
then, pure artifacts caused eternally,
time fluoresces and the dream is to know.

3.

You are an edifice deep in the soul,
yet, my silence, a thousand golden tiles
are your eves: stable treasure and simple
temple to Minerva, a massy calm
and evident restraint, an eye that guards
in you such sleep beneath a veil of flame.

4.

Temple of time, in a sole sigh resumed,
to this pure point I climb and accustom
myself, surrounded by my marine gaze.
Like a holocaust to the gods, the supreme
that I can offer, the serene brilliance
sews in the sky a sovereign disdain.

5.

Like the fruit that melts in your enjoyment,
in your mouth where its form must die, changing
into delight its own absence, here I
scent my smoky future, while heaven sings
of changing shorelines and their murmuring
to the soul that has been wholly consumed.

6.

Beautiful sky, true sky, watch as I change!
After so much pride, after idleness
so strange and yet so full of potency,
I abandon myself to this shining
space. Over houses of the dead my shadow
passes, conforming me to its frail drift.

7.

Admirable justice of light, in arms,
void of pity: I bear you, and my soul
supine below the torches of solstice.
I give you back pure to your origin:
Look at yourself… But to give back the light
is to rely on shadow's sad aspect.

8.

For myself only, alone, in myself,
next the heart, at the poem's springs, between
the emptiness and eventuation,
I await my inscape's echo, something
bitter, a sonorous unsounded well,
a reverberation always future.

9.

Do you know, pretend prisoner of leaves,
ravening beyond these meager arbors,
your secrets bursting upon my closed eyes—

Do you know, sea, this body that drags me
to its lazy end in bony earth? Sparks
in the wind, my thoughts of friends departed.

10.
Closed, holy, full of a matterless fire,
a terrestrial fragment made over
to the light, this place pleases me; composed
of gold and of stones, of somber bowers,
so much marble trembling over shadows;
and the sea is faithful, sleeps on my tombs.

11.
May the idolater cower far off!
I come solitary, with a shepherd's
smile, and I graze my mysterious sheep
a long time, my white flock of tranquil tombs.
Splendid and brutal, my dog will banish
cautious doves, vain dreams, curious angels!

12.
Arrived here, the future is idleness.
The piercing insect scratches at the drought;
everything is burnt, unmade, taken up
into what harsh essence I do not know…
Life is vast, drunk as it is on absence,
and bitterness is sweet, the mind is clear.

13.
The hidden dead are truly in this earth
that swaddles them, dries out their mystery.
Noon up high, noon without trace of movement,
thinks itself in perfect identity.
Head crowned with an absolute diadem:
I am your secret mutability.

14.

You have only me to contain your fears!
My penance, my doubts, my limitations—
the expression of your diamond flaw.
But locked in their night heavy with marble,
an unclear people among the winding roots
has already turned slowly to your cause.

15.

They have melted down into dense absence,
the red clay has drunk the pallid species
and life's gift has passed into the flowers.
The dead forget their typical phrases,
their personal art—even their unique
souls? I know the worm crawls where tears once flowed.

16.

The cry of a girl when you tickle her,
her smiling teeth, her eyes looking at you
with a leaping look, or her damp eyelids,
her heart that plays with fire, the blood that glows
in lips that give up a kiss, her utmost
gifts: all interred and returned—to the game!

17.

And you, soul, do you hope to dream a dream
finally freed of the lying colors
that these waves and their gold make for the eyes?
When you become nothing but a vapor
will you still sing? All flees; all presence is
porous; sacred impatience also dies.

18.

Thin immortality, feeble, ornate,
comforter terrible and laureate,

you make of death a mother's breast, you lie
with a pretty lie and a pious ruse.
Whoever knows, refuses the empty
grinning skull and its eternal laughter.

19.

Deep fathers, you whose heads are deserted,
you who, buried beneath the soil of spade
after spade, confound our steps—you are safe.
The true worm does not trouble you who sleep
beneath a gravestone. No. He lives off life,
there is no living hour that he leaves me.

20.

Is this love or hatred he shows for me?
Nothing is more intimate than his tongue.
I can give him any name, it does not
matter. He sees, wishes, dreams and touches,
my flesh pleases him and even in bed
to this live nothing I live to belong.

21.

Zeno! You are cruel in your paradox,
you've struck me through with your arrow that flies
and fails to fly, it quivers and is still.
I'm born of its vibrant air, and I die
when the arrow strikes. Sunlight shows Achilles's
shadow striding helpless after Tortoise.

22.

No! Enough. There is another era,
summer always arriving. Break, body,
this pensive form; drink, heart, the birth of wind.
The sea is salt and power, and will breathe
a coolness that will give me back my soul:
we'll turn and run again into the crashing foam.

23.

Yes! Great sea, dowered with delirium,
panther's hide, imperial mantle pierced
by ten thousand idols of the sun, you
transcendent hydra, drunk on your own blue,
who bite your own encircling tail, and swirl
in a self-chasing tumult like silence—

24.

The wind is up!... And we must try to live.
The air's immense; opens, closes my book.
The waves spray and dare to spout from the rocks.
All my dazzled pages—fly away now.
Break, waves, with scintillant joy break the calm
azure plain where jibs are pecking like doves.

Garden Gate

Therese Schroeder-Sheker

> *"Everything depends on grace."*
> —The Mystical Ark[1]
> *"I have been coming to this morning light since the day I was born."*[2]
> —W. S. Merwin

Beholding: My apprenticeship to *beholding* was "begun" by virtue of an empty basket waiting to be refilled and the seemingly "chance" ringing of an old-fashioned desk phone. If my mother hadn't stepped away to answer that phone call and take time to refill her laundry basket, I would have remained under the umbrella of her protective gaze and verbal instruction. As it was, by virtue of the seemingly ordinary, I discovered myself anew precisely because I was briefly entrusted to the wisdom of the garden.

Perfect Largesse: While sitting on the ground, some aperture occurred, and surely it was a sacred one. I received what was offered and found myself in a solitude unfolding by grace. In this condition, I became aware of being accompanied by a different order of guidance other than the one acknowledged by the roles shouldered by parents. The perfect largesse of Mother Nature's protection and her vast curriculum introduced (me to) new rela-

tionships *not born of physical blood*. In retrospect, I can say now that beings and creatures were present for this encounter and in the aperture I witnessed their presences along with their movements and teeming life processes. My mother's brief stepping away conveyed nothing resembling what one could call absence or negligence. It was the opposite. Presence abounded. Be that as it may, this event constituted my first conscious memory, or at least the biographical moment in which I began to be aware of listening-responding-communicating as an "I am."

> *"Marveling we venerate and venerating we marvel."*
> The Mystical Ark

> *"the sound of it will make you remember."*
> W. S. Merwin

Garden as Ark: The backyard of our home on Penrose included fencing on three sides, and a gate opening to a narrow alley where wild roses tended to spill out in profusion. A few mild-mannered bees hovered and hummed. This was not a manicured yard. The borders had abundant overgrowth that hadn't been trimmed for

---

[1] Richard of St. Victor, *The Mystical Ark: Benjamin Major*, 149–370, translated by Grover Zinn for *The Classics of Western Spirituality* (Mahwah, NJ: Paulist Press, 1979).
[2] W. S. Merwin, *Garden Time* (Port Townsend, WA: Copper Canyon Press, 2016).

some time. It was cozy that way, preferred, and the brightly colored tulips contrasting with the greenery disguised the physical fences. Instead of walls demarcating property lines, a child experienced a sweet haven or a simple, protected enclosure. Last but not least, the yard featured a magnificent oak tree, one whose girth exceeded the combined arm span of three squealing siblings when they circled it hand-to-hand. The canopy the tree provided created a shade that was regal and refreshing. The rustling of the oak's leaves on branches high and low wafted like sheets of humming voices. Sound congealed as if in a cloud formation being filled with overtones rather than rain. This resounding moved effortlessly, in the way that the sound of a choir in *pianissimo* might move from one shore to another if it were gliding over and across an inland pond.

"*We ascend to contemplation
of invisible things by means
of visible things.*"
THE MYSTICAL ARK

"*there is no other voice or time.*"
W. S. MERWIN

Ordinary Time: The aperture I want to describe required the ordinariness of a Midwestern morning, late enough in the season for the final traces of yellow, rose, and salmon colored tulips to speckle the greenery. Even so, the school term was in session. This meant that with my father at the research center and siblings in their classrooms, a mother and her youngest daughter were home together in a corridor of serenity. The two of us were outside in this backyard haven where squirrels were scampering, and sparrows, robins, and blue jays flitted from branch to branch.

Aperture: My mother had been hanging freshly washed clothes on the line to dry. I had been playing nearby, sitting on the ground close to a sandbox, easily able to see both my mother and the oak tree. The two of us were fully occupied with our separate kinds of handiwork, and life seemed to be unburdened. I was happily doing whatever it is that little ones do with a small pail, a mound of last season's acorns, and bits of bark and twigs. My mother was just about to go back inside to wring out another load of laundry for the basket when the jingling phone perforated the quiet. *Sound!* Her summons and routine chores suddenly left me differently situated. *No adult!* After she stepped away it was as if the sky had metamorphosed so that another layer or world could gradually precipitate. A quickening began to infuse the enclosure. Even now, it is difficult to find a viable way to describe it, other than to say that a new condition *emerged*, permeated by currents of warmth and fire light.

"*aided by divine showings.*"
THE MYSTICAL ARK

"*only once and only to look at
…not to touch or hold.*"
W. S. MERWIN

Epiphany: It was in this suffused tranquility that two spiritual beings precipitated alongside the oak tree. They were silent and appeared to be composed of radiant currents in continual movement. They hovered in the air and together they held a scroll or a banner between them, allowing it to roll open. The scroll contained content that was alive rather than inert. I understood the "writing" on the scroll to be a message, but had not yet learned how to read or write the letters of the alphabet. This content wasn't like the handwriting I had seen my sisters "do" on paper each night when they sat down at the dining room table to tackle their schoolwork.

The Book of Nature: Even the scroll itself appeared to be living. I say that for two reasons. First, because the "words" on it appeared to be germinating as if the fabric of the scroll were a medium like soil. Second, the "words" were quivering, pulsating and streaming, moving vertically, up and down, not "fixed" or static on the page as are our words today. I remember an urgency—a fire rising in my throat—I wanted to "read" the "words" and couldn't, yet neither could I cry out. Perceiving my struggle, the remedy came in a singular gesture of kindness.

One of the two beings silently pointed away from the scroll and toward the oak. I looked to my left and saw that the outer layer of bark on the tree conveyed or broadcast not only a signature, but a living language: the bark too was vital, teeming, *in flux*, not unlike the blossoming content visible within the scroll. As my own straining dissolved, struggle was replaced by tranquility. Time became elastic. The tree became increasingly transparent and offered entrée to its own depth. I witnessed currents

inside the oak ascending and descending like a circulatory system whose heartbeat related to the sun. Sap was tree-blood, only this blood was variously colored amber and gold and green-gold, not ruby like yours and mine.

"some of those things can be brought down for the understanding of all."
THE MYSTICAL ARK

"lent to me for part of a season."
W. S. MERWIN

Ensouled Acceptance: That very morning, I understood that both scroll and oak offered a kind of otherworldly supra-handwriting, a living-breathing-spiritual handwriting, in that both scroll and oak presented worlds that were meant to be "entered" and "read." Though sensitive enough to register subtleties, and still seated on the ground, I could not yet "read" either Nature's tree or the celestial broadcast delivered by the two. Knowing no other way to respond, I surrendered to *resting inside a wide-awake beholding* that was permeated by awe. Decades later, I recognize that this surrender was not a passivity but an active and ensouled acceptance, an implicitly pure trust, and these initial responses set the tone for essentials that would bear fruit years later.

Transmission: After some or many moments—it is hard to say which—my mother returned and hastily brought me inside after I had tried to say something about the visitation. Though the aperture closed and stopped streaming, a deep internal imprint or signature remained. The event *sealed* itself in me, into the fabric of my being, so it is safe to say that *beholding built the ark*. Though only a child, I knew in an unburdened way that the content shown was real. In retrospect, as an elder, that morning doesn't appear to me as a single seminal event, but, rather, within the quality of a transmission, one in which breathing mediates disclosure. In this case, the transmission pointed to the essential and eternal nature of covenant, and planted a variety of seeds in me that would rest for a necessary cycle of winters yet germinate in seasons to come.

"neither a light nor an easy thing
for the human soul to assume."
THE MYSTICAL ARK

"they took their light with
them when they went."
W. S. MERWIN

Closing the Portal: For quite some time after that, when my sisters sat at the dining room table in the evenings to do their school work, I would pull up a chair as if to join them. This wasn't mere imitative adoration of the big girls. I wanted to recall this beholding that happened near the oak tree and commit it to paper. Using pencil and color, I scribbled incomprehensibly across multiple pages, attempting signs and symbols that pleased no-one and made my mother nervous. Perhaps she understood the seminal origin of her daughter's hieroglyphs, and feared, pensively, what something like that could mean in a life if left to flourish unchecked. In her attempt to protect me from

anything uncanny, or maybe to make things manageable, my mother decided to do her utmost to close and lock the door to prevent the further availability of the traffic between worlds to her daughter.

She did it in an Irish way, with urgency, immediacy, and definition. She had been helping my sisters with their spelling and grammar, and so was at the table with us. There was a moment when I cried out in dismay and frustration, not being able to write or draw that other-worldly script. At this point, she furrowed her brow, came to my side and crumpled the papers. She held my face in her two hands and looked me squarely in the eye.

"Hush, child! *Hush!* 'Twas only a *dream."*

I knew it was not, yet instinctively sensed the wisdom of containment. What had happened had really happened and had come unbidden. It came amidst the ordinary, came in daylight waking hours and not while I was sleeping or dreaming. That being said, I most definitely chose to lay to rest any temptation to protest or argue. Those routes only attract unwanted attention and unleash more parental anxiety. Sometimes silence serves a condition resembling peace even when there is an undertow of unease. In this way, when talk ended and even echo died down, my very gifted mother might have been able to tell herself that the oak tree was a single bleed-through anomaly, and that Lethe had healed her child from a life of suffering and questioning. I was content to simply let things be. It may have looked like I had forgotten, but appearances and realities differ.

Agency: It is true that the tree became solid and opaque again, but beholding by grace had sealed itself into the beholder. A powerful voice of authority had insisted that something real did not happen and could not exist, and from this I began to intuit how trying it can be to be a loving and protecting parent. Still, the decree didn't cohere with the experience, so I chose to remember and honor both from a quiet ledge, a periphery, rather than from a fraying or imploding center. The collision between power and perception was something I would encounter again in adulthood, in studying the history of science, the history of biomedicine, and that of theology. Be that as it may, in childhood, voluntarily keeping mum at the right time and for the right reason, I had no experience of being silenced. Even a youngster has agency; I used mine to give assent to voluntary silence, and agency is a great mystery.

 I didn't know it then, but came to know later: If sustained, the heat of a voluntarily chosen silence concentrates itself and ripens over time. It gathers force and bears fruit. If given the chance, it operates from within a form and becomes an alchemical retort in which one's accumulated material can begin to change. Slowly, gradually, our leaden dross undergoes metamorphosis, creates an opening on the next level and centers one inside paradox: *the lead is slowly and quietly transformed into gold.*

There are times when the very thing that could be interpreted by another as a structure of diminishment or a structure of suppression can in fact gradually be disclosed as the source of an almost transcendent opposite: *Strength! Protection! Aid!* Containment asked me to go inward and to go inward deeply: in and down. That was it. Or at least part of it.

Resonance: Over time, the sustained *praxis* of containment taught me much about the ways and means of transformation, of transformative currents, and of attunement. I learned that freely-given-assent anchors one particularly and broadcasts at a particular frequency. Each frequency range activates resonance in other beings, events, and conditions. These potentize openings and movements to and fro, betwixt and between, above and below, right and left. By the same token, any given frequency range can evoke nothing more than a dull "thud" in a differently tuned milieu. If it is possible to matriculate in a wisdom curriculum prior to donning a school uniform, I was, by virtue of the garden oak, an inadvertent early enrollee. The largesse of Mother Nature had indicated a resonance path for me that would mature in a future stage.

Metabolizing this into essentials has been generative.

It is clear (to me) that if at some turning point in life we forgo something *of the moment* in lieu of something *of the eternal*, we can be issued a metaphysical passport. This seems to be a thing of rose-gold, mysteriously granting passage, allowing one to move and communicate *and* to be clothed in multiple intimate relationships, one of them being with *Natura* as being.

"some learn this by a showing while others believe and prove it incontestably by authority."
The Mystical Ark

*"your note is the time of
your radiance"*
W. S. Merwin

Noun to Verb – Event to Capacity:
How often we enter into a life-changing experience without yet having a fractional understanding of its meaning or significance, message, or mantle. Just think of relationships and life events: a teacher, a book, marriage, parenting, fire and flood. In this way, a single enigmatic hour, even in childhood, can distill into focus and become a guiding light for years of future inner work, study, prayer, reflection, meditation, and contemplation. That gradual decades-long ripening is the process of metamorphosis[3] and, simultaneously, is when and how a noun can become a verb, and an event or an experience can blossom and become a capacity.

Be assured, Dear Reader: The childhood aperture on Penrose closed and closed for good reason, but the witnessing of *Natura* as *being* rather than Nature as a *thing* sealed itself into my personhood and shaped both memory and perception.

That which is known by heart is ensouled and embodied. That kind of knowing can constellate a metaphysical compass which provides trustworthy direction if we choose to call upon it. The fabric of beholding and witnessing formed in me the fundamen-

tals needed to develop the capacity for recollection. For me, recollection gradually became grounded, by choice, within the Eucharist.

*"They worried only about Immanent
Disaster, so for the most part they
were pleasant enough."*
René Char[4]

"The opposite of security is peace."
Dietrich Bonhoeffer[5]

Terra Firma – Terra Nova: Written reflection on an experience of this nature entails an element of risk, to the degree that there are those who insist on the concrete by dismissing the metaphysical and spiritual. That being said, life has taught me that there are multiple simultaneous ways of knowing, that reality is textured and layered, and that understanding comes over time, gradually, as a sort of *costly grace*.[6] Returning to the memory of the Penrose aperture has remained a constant meditation throughout my adult life. Whether in silence, in speech, at harp, in prayer, whether in illness or in health, working inside or working outdoors, *beholding* is entrée. *Beholding* builds a metaphysical ark, a *currach* for earth, air, fire and water; a vehicle of land, sea or sky; liberating

[3] See Goethe, *The Metamorphosis of Plants*, introduction and photography by Gordon L Miller (Cambridge, MA: MIT Press, 2009). Goethe, *The Metamorphosis of Plants*, 2nd revised edition (East Troy, WI: Bio-Dynamic Literature, 1978). Gertraud Goodwin, *Metamorphosis: Journeys Through Transformation of Form* (Forest Row, UK: Temple Lodge, 2016).

[4] Rene Char, *The Smoke That Carried Us, Selected Poems*, trans. Susanne Dubroff (Buffalo, NY: White Pine Press, 2004).
[5] Dietrich Bonhoeffer, *Love Letters from Cell 92, the Correspondence between Dietrich Bonhoeffer and Maria von Wedemeyer 1943–45*, ed. Ruth-Alice von Bismarck and Ulrich Kabitz (Nashville, TN: Abingdon Press, 1995).
[6] Dietrich Bonhoeffer, *Cost of Discipleship* (Touchstone, 1995) is considered a Christian classic.

perception of warmth, light, sound and life. Most essentially, *beholding* disclosed (for me) three distinct strata embedded in a single terrain.

The three together—Garden, Gardening, and Gardener—appeared *in new and living ways*[7] that are (for me) closely tied to the monastic vision of purity of heart.[8] By the time I became an adult capable of cultivating a garden, I had also become sensitive to clusters of three and to how and why they could support the emergence of purity of heart. Wherever this signature of three-ness appeared, whenever this *trinitarian quality* permeated an endeavor or a way of being, a person or a commitment, a dialogue or path of discovery, I trusted the three together as a sign of accountability leading to understanding. Stated differently, the trinitarian cluster indicated to me *solid ground* and *new land*.

"*Poetry will rob me of my death.*"
RENÉ CHAR

"*The Word in the desert.*"
T.S. ELIOT [9]

Exemplars: "*Try to recover your natural unity,*" the Trappist Cistercian Thomas Merton[10] taught. These six words are so brief as to be easily overlooked. They may appear as mild admonition or may be received as quiet encouragement. Regardless, they constitute a very fundamental and tall order, one which Thomas Berry[11] called *the great work*, meaning: the work of a life-time.

And then we have Hans Urs von Balthasar,[12] who urgently advocated the wisdom of *keeping the three Transcendentals of Truth, Beauty and Goodness together; to separate any one from the other two*, he taught, *unleashes a kind of interpretive violence in the world.* This conviction offers a model of holiness and wholeness that is neither doctrinal, dogmatic nor abstract; it is however intrinsically agapeic and Sophianic.

Because of exemplars like Merton and von Balthasar, the imagination I began to hold as a personal ideal formed as an amalgam of their two insights. To take both seriously, meaningfully, integrally and authentically, I had to begin to cultivate a greater sensitivity and responsivity to trinities and then also apply that trinitarian tuning into daily life. First, I had to

---

[7] *Letter to the Hebrews*, chapter 10: 19–25 from the Pauline milieu, NASB.

[8] Thomas Merton, *The Silent Life*, essay "Puritas Cordis (Purity of Heart)" (New York: Farrar, Straus & Giroux, 1957).

[9] T.S. Eliot, *Four Quartets*, "Burnt Norton V" (New York: Harcourt Brace, 1943).

[10] Thomas Merton, *The Inner Experience: Notes on Contemplation*, edited by William Shannon (Harper: San Francisco, 2003). However, the editor Shannon clarifies that *The Inner Experience* was written in 1959 and that Merton edited and made minor corrections in 1968. "Try to recover your basic natural unity, to reintegrate your compartmentalized being into a coordinated and simple whole and learn to live as a unified human person. This means that you have to bring back together the fragments of your distracted existences that when you say 'I' there is really someone present to support the pronoun you have uttered."

[11] Thomas Berry, *The Great Work: Our Way into the Future* (Three Rivers Press, 1999). Also, Thomas Berry, *The Dream of the Earth* (Oakland, CA: Sierra Club 1988).

[12] Hans Urs von Balthasar, *Bernanos: An Ecclesial Existence* (San Francisco, CA: Communio-Ignatius Press, 1988).

grow to appreciate that not all dualities constellate complementarity. Good-bad; black-white; Christian-Jewish; blue collar-white collar. Some dualities activate resistance, can be polarized into opposites, one sparring for primacy over the other: *self-limiting*. Later, I grew to observe that a trinity presents a different energetic and communication dynamic: *Balance!*

Trinities are not confined to the Father, Son and Holy Spirit of Christian Tradition. Once the scales fall from the eyes, it is natural to see how available, awakening and frequent trinitarian clusters are. From this, I began to understand that there is such a thing as *trinitarian perception*. A few of the trinities that light up for me arise from different levels of being and foci, such as: body-soul-spirit; truth-beauty-goodness; thinking-feeling-willing; inflammation-homeostasis-sclerosis; love-lover-beloved; prayer-meditation-contemplation; salt-sulphur-mercury; awakening-purgation-illumination; loving-knowing-sensing; giving-waiting-receiving; excess-proportion-deficiency; soundboard-harmonic curve-pillar.

Wherever your eyes rest or thoughts land, attention and intention cry out to protect the unity of these trinities in order to move or live in balance. To separate the sound board of the harp from its pillar and harmonic curve is to destroy the instrument and silence its voice. In the same way that separating one from the other two unleashes a kind of violence against sound, preserving the interconnected and balanced unity of a trinitarian insight offers the beholder a re-imagination of wholeness that is more stable than tottering.

The Genius of Benedict: The insight about the virtue of a three-fold balance was lauded by St. Benedict as early as the sixth century and integrated into his monastic vision. He knew about the failures of religious ascetic extremes[13] from observing human foibles within religious community life itself and from reading Cassian's *Conferences*.[14] Both Cassian and Benedict understood that one cannot grow spiritually by avoiding the body or by bypassing the soul. Within the shelter of *purity of heart*, praying ceaselessly models an attitude, gesture, consciousness and praxis and yet differs greatly from an "ascetic one-upmanship that pursued physical disciplines[15] as if they were ends in themselves." To the extent that any fasting, prayer, or vigil effort emerged as a disembodied extreme, the elders noted that those choices fueled competition and/or resentment in community as well as self-deception, vanity or inflation in the heart of the individual practitioner. Benedict advised practical, tranquil and pro-active solutions in *structures* of balance and structures of proportion, ones that, if integrated, are astonishingly creative and generous. He advised that the day be structured so that each of the three kinds of dimensions were faithfully lived and practiced, all in the spirit of service. Each person engages

---

[13] The Symeon the Stylite and Syrian stylite asceticism both come to mind.
[14] John Cassian, *Conferences*, translation and preface Colm Luibheid and Introduction by Owen Chadwick, in *The Classics of Western Spirituality* series (Mahwah, NJ: Paulist Press, 1985).
[15] William Harmless, S.J., *Desert Christians: An Introduction to the Literature of Early Monasticism* (Oxford: Oxford University Press, 2004).

in some form of manual physical labor along with some form of intellectual or artistic work along with specific forms of inner work and prayer. There was nothing disembodied, unensouled or spiritually anemic about Benedict's ideal. However short of the mark individuals and communities have historically fallen and will surely continue to fall from this three-fold ideal, aiming for body, soul and spirit balance remains one of the strongest traditional aspirational characteristics of Benedictine life.

Challenges and Obstacles: In my experience, Benedict's three-fold balance is a staggeringly difficult path of commitment to inhabit in a highly technological post-industrial, postmodern corporate world. I say that because the contemporary maladies of fragmentation and compartmentalization are rampant regardless of work environment, community, vocation or career. Not everyone is intimate with the grounding and metabolizing gifts that can accompany physical manual labor. On the one hand, I know few doctors, lawyers or abbots who work in a garden, large or small. On the other, we read daily of millions of people toiling under demoralizing conditions that accompany the treatment of the earth as a commodity, a source of profit. In between the two extremes, we have the new wave of individuals and communities who are living a sustainable vision that aspires toward balance.

Walking the Talk: With these layers in mind, Garden became a linchpin for me in light of incarnational spirituality. It was as much a focal reality

about balance as the hearth is to the warmth of the home. For John Cassian, the monastic vocation didn't defer beatitude to an afterlife but sought to see God[16] *here and now—to get a glimpse, however brief, however tentative, of heaven on earth.* Garden: an archetypal reality, never a hobby, perhaps a Transcendental, a constant inspiration, a path of beauty, a wellspring of nurturing health, a path embracing *Natura*, a sacramental path offering further participation in the Mystical Body, and finally, an extension of Eucharist.

So this is how and why Garden (noun, verb and being) became a critical element in my own grounding—intrinsic to an incarnational spirituality, in the contemplative life, in the capacity to walk the talk, to demonstrate what we hear and say about the most essential messages of the Gospels: the Word of Christ. Everything we know and love is on loan, and surely the privilege of gardening could be lost or taken away in times to come; but at this point, with Garden, with the inclusion of manual labor into the fullness of daily life, I am able to live more fully and move more genuinely toward the Benedictine ideal of balance.

"Love does not dominate; it cultivates."
GOETHE, *Das Märchen*[17]

Citizen of the Planet: It has been a blessing to have had the opportunity to live and work in many different places and situations in several parts of the world, and to experience a wide

16 Ibid.
17 Johann Wolfgang von Goethe, *Maxims and Reflections* (General Books Club, 2010).

spectrum of ecosystems—remote forests and inland rivers; mountains and prairies; shorelines and brooks; scrublands and grasslands; metropolitan cities and obscure hamlets. Travel can allow us to experience gardens tended by humans and gardens born of unsung elements and invisible hands.

Having cherished both, I have lived, worked and gardened in hermetic hideaways free of noise and light pollution—and these acres were further protected and amplified because they bordered miles of environmentally protected greenbelt. I have also lived and worked in the noisiest and most populated of European and American cities, places that had been bombed during World War II, places where cement rules the day, places where one works hard to get an afternoon off to walk in a city park designed by landscape architects. Life has allowed me to live, learn, work and flourish on large and small farms and in large and small gardens and to root and thrive in an opposite: the one-room, third-story apartment nook where a single gabled window ledge serves as the altar for a potted plant. Each situation offered its own kind of heaven and apprenticeship. These days, and for the previous decade, I garden in a small enclosure in a quiet village.

Outdoor Physical Labor: I am less physically strong now than when younger, but remain inspired by all the garden has to offer and teach. It has been a joy and a privilege to be healthy enough to continue to work outside in a physical manner and to be able to alternate that physicality with the more interior (and indoor) activities of music, scholarship, clinical work,

teaching. That being said, prayer is integrated into both indoor and outdoor ways of being. When in the priory garden, I am able to do some intensely physical manual labor outdoors almost daily, carrying soil or rock by the sweat of the brow; planting, watering, pruning, transplanting, cultivating, harvesting, and caring for an oddly shaped garden and a humble orchard. Even in the winter, the Pacific Northwest with its Mediterranean climate allows for a mild amount of outdoor work. However great or humble the patch of earth being tilled, to be able to work and garden seriously *outdoors* while also maintaining a second work-life *indoors* has evolved (for me) as a much needed complementarity. It has provided me with a rich set of contrasts and learning tools. Intimacy with both choices has helped me form vital questions and make new connections that could not have arisen (for me) in abstraction. The inclusion of physical manual labor into the opus has helped me re-imagine life, holiness, health and wholeness in ways that tend to upend and dissolve widely held assumptions about success. I can't take credit for this, as the re-imagination did not arise unaided. It has been mediated by the wisdom of exemplars.

> "All at once there arose in my hearth a battle of embers never to subside again."
> RENE CHAR

> "throw roses at everyone"
> EDITH SÖDERGRAN [18]

---

[18] Edith Södergran, *Complete Poems*, translated by David McDuff (Bala, North Wales: Bloodaxe Books, 1984).

The Litany of Descriptors: During many years of scholarship, I discovered evocative terms[19] that emerged from different historical cultures spanning a large arc of time. Listen to their names ring! *Enclosed garden, temple garden, Druidic garden, monastic garden, Cistercian garden, rose garden, culinary garden, herb garden, medicinal garden, Ficino's garden, Goethe's garden, alchemical garden, memorial garden, Zen garden, manor garden, country garden, urban garden.* As I encountered the descriptors, they resounded and appeared like welcoming heralds. Each descriptor shed additional light on the sources of inspiration and motivation that kindled manual labor through the ages, coupled with a relationship to Natura as being. Together, the various heralds fired my own imagination of healing, holiness and wholeness, and offered a different way of participating in the Mystical Body of Christ.

"*Be accustomed to walking in heavenly places with dwellers in heaven.*"
THE MYSTICAL ARK

"*stars gone into another life*"
W. S. MERWIN

The Memorial Garden: The enclosed garden in which I work is intentionally small and beautifully intentional. In it, over a hundred kinds of fruits, flowers, herbs, and vegetables flourish in a small area. The most mysterious voice amongst the prolific greening comes from a section I call the memorials, and in this case, the alchemical priory memorials.

During the Last Supper, and in our contemporary celebration of the Eucharist, we cherish the fact that Christ tells the devoted to "do this in memory of me." If we think about doing anything in memory of Him, or something in memory of any beloved person *let alone the Master*, the act of remembering has the potential to emerge as a sacramental bridge, linking heaven and earth.

"*That difference which is between wood and gold is the difference between the historical and spiritual senses of Scripture.*"
THE MYSTICAL ARK

"*Memory alone is awake with me.*"
W. S. MERWIN

The monastic customaries show that the traditional Benedictine Cluniac *charism* of connecting the communities of the living with the communities of the dead was an important contribution to every dimension of culture.[20] It was natural then for me to pray in that tradition, praying daily in memory of loved ones and apparent strangers, all of whom Joa Bolendas[21] calls the Risen Ones. Sometimes

---

[19] See *Medieval Gardens* edited by Elizabeth B. Macdougall (Dumbarton Oaks Research Library and Collection at Harvard, 1986), but especially "The Medieval Monastic Garden" by Paul Meyvaert.

[20] Therese Schroeder-Sheker, *Transitus: A Blessed Death in the Modern World* (West Scarborough, ME: St. Dunstan's Press, 2001). Also, Frederick Paxton, *Christianizing Death* (Ithaca, NY: Cornell University Press, 1990).
[21] Joa Bolendas, *So That You May Be One* (Great Barrington, MA: Lindisfarne Books, 1997) and Joa Bolendas, *Alive in God's World* (Lindisfarne Press, 2001).

this prayer expresses itself as pure thanksgiving, characterized by listening and waiting. Other times it also includes all those gestures related to asking a question, or to forgiveness and healing. With time, as if prayer prepares the garden bed, I do my best to enter silence. Only then does the choosing and planting of the memorial rose, lily, olive tree and more occur, one primary choice for each individual being remembered. A single intentional plant, bush or tree is chosen and cultivated in memory of each of their lives and life-works, each teacher and mentor, each of those who have gone on ahead of us, and for whom I am filled with gratitude. This has occupied years of inner work and manual labor, and the memorials grow in number each year as so many make their *transitus*. The memorial garden may seem like a courteous thing to do, but it is more. Being with each memorial through the seasons and years teaches me as much about spiritual alchemy as it does sacrament.

"Mystical understanding is tripartite."
  • THE MYSTICAL ARK

"Memory walking in the dark."
W. S. MERWIN

"I cannot tell you how readable the book of nature is becoming for me."
GOETHE [22]

Early in the morning, it is possible to visit and hand water or prune each of the memorial plantings while praying and listening. Yes, that means I stand close to that which has been planted for my mother, father, grandmother, family members, dearest friends, and loved ones, all my beloved teachers, especially the music teachers, several saints and consecrated individuals, and yes, Mary and John, Merton and Von Balthasar, Bach and Finzi, Hildegard and Mechthild, Plotinus and Ficino, and quite a few more. I say their names internally and out loud, to let each ring in my soul as well as in the physical air, and each memorial is labeled with the individual's name. These "labels" are specially made by a local sign-maker who understands that his work is contributing to a prayer praxis. He told me once that he too is praying internally when he creates each sign for this garden. Usually at the foot of a memorial tree, there will be a secondary choice, almost always an herb. Each plant is intentional and alchemical, often unlikely but not arbitrary. The total effort might combine a berry with a labiate, or a drupe with a *rosaceae*.

To the extent that the bridge between worlds has been cultivated and cherished as a sacramental possibility, a certain expressive communion can take place in these quiet dawn and dusk hours devoted to memorial garden prayer and to the vocation of gardening. Something is emerging that has the quality of an office of hours for the manual laborer.

There is also a section reserved for those who have committed suicide, for as the years pass, from my own time as a college student to the present, we see that suicide[23] rates have increased dramatically. There are

[22] *The Metamorphosis of Plants*, op. cit.

[23] See the David Leonhardt and Stuart A Thompson opinion piece published in *The*

several such lives and souls remembered in the memorial garden. We love and cherish these people, without hesitation, and surely they benefit from being remembered faithfully. Observing each of their memorials allows me to say generally that their processes seem to unfold outside of time. When one of them suddenly flowers, or exudes a glorious fragrance, particularly after years of dormancy, my heart just about leaps in my chest and I am down on my knees in praise and thanksgiving.

Sometimes there are individuals who struggled with one another during life, or hurt or betrayed one another when they were alive, and if or when their two individual memorial plants or trees suddenly blossom or fruit on the same day, even though different species, planted far apart or close together, I know in body, soul and spirit that something powerful and alchemical is being expressed and communicated. It is important to witness this kind of potential, not to explain it or define it. Just witness it and marvel. These bits no doubt constitute an elder way of reading and entering the *Book of Nature*, and an elder way of praying, hoping, and keeping the two communities connected.

I also hope the priory garden is even a tad bit Dorothy Day subversive, because each hour bridging with the our beloved exemplars and loved ones doesn't only connect the verticality of the community of the living with the community of the dead, it is also an hour liberated from the clutches of technology.

And what about the hours that are not so rarified? There are times when you and I might only see the literal garden, joying in the fragrance and color of the herbs and fruits. These so nurture body, soul and spirit, and this is in itself already more than enough.

"unseen among the waking doves who answer from the sleep of the valley there is no other voice or other time."
W.S. MERWIN

The Presence of the Risen Christ: Because I am writing during the Coronavirus pandemic, houses of worship are closed and entire cities are on lock down. Many are grieving the sudden death of a family member or loved one. We have been told to stay home and center in solitude. We have received word of services being streamed by the various traditions, and in a precedent setting corridor, no Eucharist has been available to the Christian faithful, at least at the physical level. The sacramental caesura • exists for governmental reasons, and yet I have wondered if it might also serve a great unknown, even a mystery. Individuals who are socially distanced are describing a return to essentials. The solitude is encouraging individuals to enter into or experience a different quality of prayer and interiority *and* to express love and care in newly tender ways.[24] Perhaps this moment contains the potential to open more doors (mystical and spiri-

New York Times on March 6, 2020. "How Working-Class Life is Killing Americans." In this piece, the authors discuss the Nobel Prize winning work of Anne Case and Angus Deaton (deaths of despair).

[24] I am thinking of the singers singing across balconies.

P's!
first trust the alliteration

tual) than the physical ones the pandemic has padlocked.

There are times and conditions in the garden when the quality of the quickened air and uncanny breeze suggest that additional layers and dimensions might be available for entrée. We have always read that He will come again in the clouds. This means many things, among them: Resurrection currents permeate and potentize the very intersection of earth and sky. *The humble little square foot where you are digging right now might be nothing less than potentized ground, sacred ground, nothing less than altar.* Surely He is close at hand—*so very close.*

You startle and inhale deeply. A lone mourning dove landing at your feet, a sudden fragrance wafting without source, the lily speaking next to the rose, a hummingbird lingering at your cheek, the berries surrounded by greens, the sudden bowing of an apple tree or olive when there is in fact no wind: these arrive and invade the fertile liminal pathways in order to startle, awaken and rekindle the human heart.

"saying to myself Remember this."
W. S. Merwin

Epiclesis: At this stage of my life, when thinking about the alchemical garden or the priory garden, I cherish both mystery and miracle. Nor can I distance any of this miraculous beauty and mysterious fecundity from the part of the Eucharistic rite referred to as *epiclesis*. At the consecration, matter and spirit interpenetrate and congeal and especially so when one turns in priestly humility to thank, to raise, to offer and bless. I am more elder

now than younger, gardening in the ephemeral hours of changing light—dawn and dusk—yet always gardening in solitude. It is a joy to do so, because the garden is not a center for irritating or burdensome chores but rather a very pure context in which to pray and to share life. By extension, cultivating a garden or an orchard year after year through the changing seasons offers the gardener an embodied school of prayer. It has taken me a long time to appreciate how and why consecration occurs, whether we are acknowledging the consecration of beings or of spaces. It is possible that some receive the Risen Master in His Resurrection body more deeply while working in the garden amidst the brambles and quivering buds than when in our finest dress, while sitting indoors in a chapel or even in a Whitsun-imbued cenacle. I accept that.

"Nowhere else will you find what you can marvel at more worthily; nowhere else will you find what you can love more rightly."
The Mystical Ark

The Resurrection: These dimensions being risked in written form, no matter where I have been living or where I have been going, one vision in particular has colored and sculpted my own perception of the word "Garden," whether this Garden speaks of noun, verb, or being. The Johannine Gospel narrative describes how Jesus had been buried in a newly-hewn tomb situated *in the garden*. The word garden is repeated twice in close proximity, once to locate the crucifixion and a second time to describe the placement of the burial tomb. John further recounts

Mary Magdalene's solitary encounter with the Risen Christ early on Sunday morning. She is standing right outside the tomb. The word garden is not repeated a third time, but the way in which John places Mary, we know that Christ reveals Himself to her there *in the garden*. She is the first to whom the Master appears; He inhabits a new form, and for a moment, she mistakes Him for *the Gardener*.

Does not her "mistake" offer a timeless mystery? A blessed paradox? The strongest possible indication of what is to come? The Risen one did not choose to appear as a king or a prince or a star in the sky, but as one whose humanity could momentarily be mistaken for a gardener. The Risen Christ mirrored something precious to us about the luminous nature of work while appearing in His own radiant light-body.

And what about the mystery of perceiving the Risen One in an early morning hour? Before the hustle and bustle of the tyranny of the urgent begins to stir again? It is all there, simplicity shining through complexity.[25]

To this day, each time I work in the garden, hair askew, face surely splotched with soil, and skin dripping in perspiration, I pray in this new-old way: carrying a hope that it is embodied, ensouled, fresh, rhythmic, and knowing that it is imperfect but hope-filled, love-filled, inside joy.

This is the recollected moment where the Magdalenian possibility leaves me trembling. Who amongst us

knows how to love the way she did? Surely not I, and surely no one I know, and yet this potent model is there for each of us to approach. Surely any who might be capable of perceiving and receiving *Natura* as *living being* instead of Nature as transactional commodity is drawing near to the altar of the Eucharist and to something of Easter Sunday morning.

"it can be given but can never be sold."
W. S. MERWIN

The Claude Monet painting from 1879 entitled *Orchard in Bloom* (*Verger en Fleurs*) speaks to me of the great delicacy and the condition required for something like Mary Magdalene's seeing, Mary's Easter Morning perception. Her gaze was born of an increasingly awakened and enlarged heart torn asunder. In the painting, the blossoming of trees proliferates, and we inhale the most delicate possible fragrance and color of white petals tinged with the palest rose-hued veins. Monet's orchard hints at how it is He might have made Himself known to one nearby.

The Magdalene was with Jesus at the Cross till the very end, and when she was most disheveled, exhausted and begrimed, after two nights of sleeplessness and confusion, she saw Him, the Risen Christ, pre-dawn on Sunday morning, in spring air that is quivering in the fragrance of the blossoming trees.

In the Gospels, the Magdalene sees Him before the apostles do, demonstrating a Sophianic expression of metanoia, and showing a way of standing utterly unmasked. In the following years and millennia, many

---

[25] See Raimondo Panikkar on the monastic archetype in his Holyoke lectures of 1980 later published under the rubric of *Blessed Simplicity* by Seabury Press in 1982.

unknown others have surely followed in her perceptual footsteps by treating the Earth and Garden as sacred ground. If we enter the Monet in the spirit of prayer and or contemplation, something akin to morphic resonance occurs and the presence of the past shimmers through again. The world of blossoming petals hints at the context in which Mary might have perceived Him. A distracted or pre-occupied person would not be able to notice *Some One* standing nearby, in spirit, nor would he or she have been able to receive his or her humanity mirrored back as an archetypal gardener, one modestly engaged in manual labor.

Orchard in Bloom, Claude Monet, 1879

"Above reason yet not beyond
reason . . . by means of a divine showing."
THE MYSTICAL ARK

"This is precisely the crux of it . . . provided I myself don't forget."
IMRE KERTÉSZ[26]

"here and now – to get a glimpse, however brief, of heaven on earth."
JOHN CASSIAN

---

[26] Imre Kertész, *Fatelessness*, a new translation by Tim Wilkinson (New York: Vintage International, 2004).

The New Jerusalem: One day, when least expected, every paradox will surface and break through to higher ground. It will happen when you are most tired and yet strangely capable of radiance, perhaps you are even a little crooked and worse for the wear. You will find yourself in the garden. Despite all your partials, something whole is bleeding through your afflictions. You are recollected and cannot separate the digging and pruning from the silent praying, from the pulsing glory or thanksgiving. You are full body-soul-and-spirit praying, connected to the Mystical Body of Christ. There is an opening, either internal or external. Long ago a Magdalenian moment ushered in the new. Could something happen again?

Catching some subtle movement out of the corner of your eye, it seems, you will find yourself turning ever so slightly, your trowel caught aloft in mid-air. You are open. Turning to see and hear. Turning to witness. The quickening air. Worlds within worlds. Currents of moving light and pulsating warmth. The fragrance from the far country.

You might even hear your name.

You fall to your knees and your eyes are wet. The *Book of Revelation* suggests that the church of the New Jerusalem has no doors or windows. No walls. Open. The inside-outside dichotomy is long gone. *Natura* can receive the appearance of the Risen Christ. The chapel, the tabernacle and the garden are one. The question then is a heart-breaking mixture of humility and astonished joy: When *hasn't* He been there, so close to home, standing at the end of this flower-strewn path?

The Chalice Well Priory Garden

PENANT MELANGELL

Jon Egan

Here in this small valley,
A tiny fracture in the fabric of humdrum
In a world reduced to dead dust and numbers,
A saint once found refuge
And nature, for a moment, felt its immanent glory.

Where a shrine once venerated
now fallen into sleepy forgetfulness,
Is buried in the dreamtime of faithless Christendom.

Here something stirs.
Deeper than silence.
All of creation groans in travail
And waits in eager expectation
For a new heaven
And a new earth.

Saint John of theWilderness, Tyler DeLong

CHERRY SAPLINGS

Ruth Asch

Their congregation fills my eye:
a circle close, arms tip to tip
gracefully raised for solemn breath
before the ritual dance begin.
Their joy exhales to sun and sky
a blushed and starry innocence,
the newness of nature's delight
and awe at their own blossoming.

A PLACE TO LIVE

Jonathan Monroe Geltner

Last night I dreamed of Christ again.
He was in his twenty-ninth year.
I don't know how I knew this.
He was alone. I saw him
as he stepped out of a small cabin—
more of a shack, really—
in the shade of gentle hills
of woods and meadows.
It was not neatly constructed,
a deliberately minimal structure
like Thoreau's at Walden.
And it wasn't the profound hut
of some drunken Chinese hermit-poet.
No, it was rather the ramshackle
dwelling of a hillbilly, a shithole in the sticks.
The kind of building that has never
looked good, the kind of structure
where a whole class of people, a whole race—
no, many races—have lived for century
upon century without ever looking good,
without ever seeing a golden age.
The whole thing looked like it could
collapse at any minute and that—
if this were possible—
it actually wanted to collapse.
A stone chimney appeared to be the only
surviving piece of a previous homestead,
around which this newer shelter
had been haphazardly built up in lost
time past and just as helplessly let lapse
from original decrepitude into outright ruin.
Stuck together improbably and inexpertly
out of any old material: bricks, unhewn rocks,
vinyl siding, a mélange of shingles and even
straw and daub and plywood in places.
The windows were broken of course.

The door hung loose on the hinges
and swayed and creaked in the breeze.
The wooden stoop was decomposing;
on it a pile of soggy firewood looked incapable
of giving warmth. It was creepy, the kind of place
where if you were lost in the woods, even in winter,
and you came upon it, you might not knock,
for fear that it was some sociopath's
boondocks methlab.
In a slightly less decadent age
you might have expected to see a still around back.
But at least there was no truck.
No rusting automobile of any kind,
not even parts of one. No driveway,
not so much as a gravel or a dirt path.
I felt he'd been living here
a little while.
            And Christ, stepping out,
looked much as you would expect a man to look
who lived in such a place.
His hair was long and wavy, matted and mud-colored—
almost shiny for all the grease. His beard
was totally unkempt. Not that adolescent fur
you see in most of the western iconography—
the ineffectual effort of a college sophomore
trying to impress a girl and pass
for twenty-one at the corner liquor store.
It was a serious, thick, curly, deep brown mane.
But he stood straight upright, his shoulders squared.
He tasted the air with a long breath.
It was cool outside—autumn—
but he wasn't wearing much.
I think his pants were of deerskin,
like his archaic moccasins, and besides this
he had only a coarse and thick woolen shirt.
He slung a small leathern sack over his back
and I knew it contained his lunch.
It was a simple meal, a hunk of dark bread,
a raw brown onion, a little wheel of white cheese
and a flask of red wine

(or maybe it was beer, dark as the bread).
I knew this. But where did the food come from?
I don't know. Perhaps he had a few small fields
nearby for some crops and kept a goat
or some sheep and chickens and maybe even a cow.
Or maybe he lived off the charity of a neighbor,
or bought or traded for his provisions somehow.
I can't say. I saw no animals, no vegetable patch,
just the man.
He set off with a confident, long stride,
and I saw he was going to eat his lunch
at the top of the hill, where he'd have a good view
of the sky, and the surrounding crests
and ridges and gullies in all their warm color.
And that's when it hit me, when he was walking
up the slope, that's when I was suddenly
and absolutely certain—these were my hills.
The trees I grew up with: silver- and sugar-maples,
sweetgums and oaks (red, white and a dozen other kinds),
honeylocusts and hickories and yellow poplars,
ashes and basswoods, hackberries and serviceberries,
cottonwoods and sycamores in the little valleys,
dogwoods and the odd conifer or two
(a hemlock, say, or an arborvitae),
and underneath all, here and there,
dense thickets of honeysuckle.
I smelled what he smelled, musky
buckeyes and black walnuts, limestone
and dank clayey air, and all the fecund
scent of deciduous country.
I heard what he heard: rustle and cackle
of squirrels, starling and raven and grackle,
all the birds that mean lengthening nights,
and chipmunks and bobwhites and turkeys
disturbing the forest floor
where his quiet feet passed.
The ways the hills were shaped,
with all their hollows and a creek in every one,
those soft, those erotic curves,
ghosts of old mountains—

This was my land.
                      And now Christ was sitting
in a little clearing up top, his back against
an old burned out stump.
It was a fine autumn day,
really rather mild for the lateness of the year,
yet the air was fresh and clear—
rare for that humid, riverine province.
He chomped healthily, calmly at his meal,
taking the occasional long swig from the flask:
some of the liquid would get on his beard,
where also there were crumbs,
for which he had no care.
His eyes, black and adamantine, gleamed,
staring wide at the undulant horizon.
It is time
they seemed to say. Or say, better,
they seemed full of time, full of the time
that is right for a certain kind of deed?
I don't know. But then, before I lost the dream,
I thought I understood him,
that moment of his life.

Hocking County, Ohio, June 2011

In the Kingdom of the Queen

An Interview with Gunther Hauk

Michael Martin

 UNTHER HAUK IS THE EXECUTIVE DIRECTOR of The Spikenard Farm Honeybee Sanctuary and has over forty years of experience in biodynamic farming and beekeeping. He was a gardening teacher at two Waldorf Schools in Germany for twenty-three years before returning to the United States in 1996 to co-found The Pfeiffer Center, one of the first biodynamic training centers in the country. This was the year the article "Hush of the Hives" appeared in *The New York Times*. From that point on, the bee work became ever more important to him, resulting in the founding of The Spikenard Farm Honeybee Sanctuary in 2006 and moving to Illinois with the organization onto 610 acres. The Sanctuary moved to Virginia in 2009, radically downsizing from 610 acres to 25. Since then, the Sanctuary and its pedagogical offerings have attracted not only insects and birds, but students and visitors from around the world.

Gunther's book *Toward Saving the Honeybee* (2002) was the first call nationwide for changing exploitive conventional beekeeping methods favored by conventional beekeeping. Fortunately, the movement toward bee-centric beekeeping methods is gaining momentum. His work was featured in two full-length documentary films about the honeybee crisis: *Queen of the Sun* (2010) and *Vanishing of the Bees* (2009), and he also produced his own educational film *Hour of Decision* (2015).

MM: What, in a very real sense, is a garden to you?

GH: That's a great question. For me, a garden goes beyond nature; it is culture. We are surrounded by nature, which is the wisdom and the beauty created by the Creator and his helpers—you know, the Exusiai, the Sera-phim, the Cherubim, all the hierarchies and their offspring, the elemental beings. And that is nature. There's wisdom in every tiny, tiny little bit—and beauty. To go one step further, we need to create culture: this is the step from just taking from Nature, as it was created for us, to *cultivating it*. That's the basis of culture:

human creativity and work, with a goal in mind: either a harvest or simply beauty, or both. So a garden is full of intention as well as possibilities to train qualities like patience, persistence, care, dedication and observation. And in this endeavor we can create something good and beautiful, or we can poison the earth and the waters, create feedlots. For a long time, when we were still in tune with rhythms of nature and possessed a view that went beyond the physical realm, we were able to create islands of beauty and fertility in midst of nature. Just think of the monastery gardens, of the orchards and fields cared for in such a way as to leave a better soil with more humus for the next generation. At present, in conventional farming, we are depleting the humus 80 times as fast as it can be created in nature. Gardening—and in a way I include farming—is a step from just being surrounded by the wisdom of nature to becoming co-creators. And none of what is created will be of lasting goodness if the work is lacking a deeper understanding, which is always the prerequisite for love. Only understanding the needs of the other will let us do deeds of love. Without love we can, of course, work hard at gardening and farming and achieve impressive results, but we will distance ourselves even more from farms and gardens that are sustainable or even thriving.

MM: That's what's missing from agriculture and apiculture, generally.

GH: Yes. We have invented amazing technology for achieving quicker and bigger results, cheaper prices for all that we eat and drink, but relatively few people are aware of the horrendous negative impact this has on all life forms. Presently we have lost about one quarter of all bird species in the USA, not to speak of myriads of insect species becoming extinct. Do we know that these are the all-important beings that make up the web of life?

MM: Can you say anything about the breathing of the year in terms of the garden and of the relationship of the bee to this breathing?

GH: Generally, people think of this earth as just a bunch of rocks, with plants, animals and human beings on it. An "insignificant speck of dust in the cosmos" is a phrase one can hear frequently. Few people know that this is a living organism: a living organism that breathes and has rhythms. I'm reminded that Günther Wachsmuth asked Rudolf Steiner—"I want to study life. How do I do that?" Steiner told him to study rhythms. There are actually tremendously complex rhythms on earth. A basic one is one of breathing: The earth has a short breath and a long breath. The short breath is during the day; its exhalation begins at 3:00 a.m. and lasts until noon. The inhalation begins at 3:00 p.m. and lasts until midnight. The times between are the transition times. The gardener can definitely work with—and not against—this rhythm for his advantage. You harvest lettuce in the morning and not afternoon, since it will stay crisp longer. The opposite is true for carrots. The honeybees live with the daily rhythm, but also with the long one which lasts the entire year. This long breath, from

Sagittarius to Gemini, is the out-breath of the earth, and from there to Sagittarius is the in-breath, perceived by us semi-consciously. Experience tells us when we sow a lettuce in April, we can harvest it a lot sooner than if we sow it in August. The outbreath lets the plants grow faster, the inbreath after the summer solstice draws vegetation back into the earth, first imperceptibly, and then quite strongly after the fall equinox.

The bees are in sync with that rhythm. Their exhalation, growth of the colony, begins in February—February 1st, Candlemas, when the queen starts laying eggs. Of course, there's variation: in Florida it begins a little sooner, in Canada it's a bit later. This building-up of the hive in the spring and the swarming in April, May, June is part of this exhalation. Already in July the bees are looking toward the winter; comb-building and swarming stops, and basically all the energy is spent in building up the provisions needed to survive the winter as a colony.

MM: I've noticed that even in wet years, the bees seem to get more done.

GH: Well, on a rainy day they work more on fermenting the pollen to make what is called "bee-bread," and on fermenting, condensing the nectar into honey. Of course, they wish they could fly out, because that's actually their task: to pollinate whatever needs to be pollinated, and gather nectar even if that reduces the space they have available for creating more brood. A honey-bound hive has no more room for the brood! This self-lessness is unparalleled in nature. Really, they are great examples for us.

MM: In terms of rhythms, then, what is your own rhythm in (for lack of a better term) "working with the bees"?

GH: We respect the need for real quiet in the winter cluster, because something else, not perceived by us, goes on there. It may seem outwardly quiet, but the winter forces are the inner forces of fertility that become outwardly evident in spring and summer. For the bees this quiet time is so important. I see it also, for example, with the chickens. We hardly get any eggs in December and January, but come spring, they are just bursting with laying again. This rhythm can also be observed with the bees.

The colonies are friendlier in spring, while in the fall they are more inclined to protect their winter stores and give you a sting or two. It's also good to work with a colony in the morning rather than in the late afternoon, as they are calmer and not worn out by all the flights they have made.

MM: How do you think of the feminine (even the Divine Feminine) in terms of the hive? I've read many books on beekeeping and have never seen this addressed.

GH: It took me a long time, too, to get to understanding more. Goethe, in his *Faust*, gives us the clue: "The Eternal Feminine draws us upward." The feminine, the Divine Feminine, has something to do with holding the goal of evolution in its being and giving impulses to humanity that let us come ever closer and make it possible that the goal can be achieved. In Christianity, we have the Father—that is considered to be the male quality (it has nothing to do with the sexes)—the Son is part of the Father but also contains the Holy Spirit, which stands for the feminine quality of nurturing. For me, it is also the feminine quality of knowing the goal. We sin against the Spirit when we sin against the goal of our evolution here on earth: the transformation of the cosmos of wisdom into a cosmos of love. For me that means that wisdom is raised to another level out of our free and selfless deeds of compassion, of understanding. Those are the sins that cannot be forgiven. It's really very stark and a hard pill to swallow.

MM: And that's the sin that characterizes our civilization at the moment, is it not?

GH: Right. We sin in so many ways against this Divine Feminine, which radiates the goal of evolution into the present. We live consciously, in our day consciousness, in the stream of time coming from the past right into the present. In order to perceive this other stream, coming from the future, we have to open up our hearts, we have to be able to let go of what we have achieved in the past, we have to become vulnerable and, in a sense, homeless. That's easily said but not easy to achieve out of freedom, not out of outer circumstances inflicting it on us. We have to live in trust that the future will bring to us what we need. The disciples had to do that. To not take along provisions acquired in the past: they couldn't even take any money or food with them. They had to live in trust. That's actually the Divine Feminine: trust in the future. At this time we are not thinking about

the children, the grandchildren, the future—the whole future, when we come again. If that were part of common knowledge, things would be very different. This is where Steiner puts so much emphasis and work into a Western understanding of reincarnation and karma: that we harvest whatever we sow, the good and the bad, not all in one lifetime. Unfortunately, so little of this understanding has been taken up in the general culture.

MM: There seems to be in human cultures a preoccupation—I would even call it an unhealthy preoccupation—with the past. And not even concerned with the present or the future.

GH: Yes, how much can I get in the next year or at most in five years? The problem is that we think that we only live one life and then it's all over. Once more people would know that there is a life after life, and that, in order to evolve, we need to come again and again, then we would focus more on what we do with and for nature, for each other.

MM: That would be a long-term view. But getting back to the Divine Feminine… I often point out to people that the Pentecost mood—the disciples waiting in anticipation of the coming of the Spirit—is often overlooked, but they were with the Mother of Jesus. As if she drew it down.

GH: Exactly. The Mother was present. No doubt, very important. Look at Mary Magdalene, look at the ones who first saw the Risen Christ on Earth. All of the nurturing the Mother of Jesus bestowed on him between the age of 12 and 30, helped him accomplish what he did, to be ready to receive the Spirit at the baptism.

We, too, have to work on not getting stuck on the old, on taking impulses from the future so what we can have the future that is meant to be ours. The honeybees are such a great example for this ability of giving up all they have worked for and going with trust into the future. They do that every time they swarm, leaving all they have built up in past year and taking provisions for only three days along with them. Since only about 25% of swarms survive in nature, their gift—a young queen and a complete hive—is the sacrifice they make for the future. What an ideal to strive for: absolutely no guarantee, in complete trust that they will be taken care of. This is the Divine Feminine, the Holy Spirit.

MM: It leads us ever onward.

GH: And the terrestrial feminine can throw some real roadblocks there.

MM: That actually leads to my next question. I cannot help but think of the honeybee as a signifier of our human condition: that the current suffering and pathologies in the bee society mirror those in human society. Can you speak to this?

GH: The bees actually represent the best in us. We have the whole animal realm in us on the soul level: we have the sloth in us, the stubborn ass, the ferocious lion, the hamster... we have all of that as a potential. The bees, in their focused diligence and their working for the well-being of all of

nature's future, their selflessness... they do live those qualities that, if we can live them, represent the best in us. And that is exactly what is being thrown out at this time: "get whatever you can and as fast as possible." Yes, we are diligent, but how much of that diligence is for creating a good future? The courtesy, the civil conversation, the humility... the truth: all of that is under serious attack. The atmosphere of greed, of deceit and lies, has become the norm, though fortunately not for everyone. That's actually the pollutant nobody talks about. We think about the physical pollutants, but that's actually the major pollutant that affects the bees and all of life. The honeybees, they're subjected to the greed of commercial beekeeping, to the plastic foundation, the sugar or corn syrup feeding, and to all the agents of death (-icides) that are being used—pesticides, insecticides, fungicides, herbicides—the bees suffer tremendously from the physical abuse as well as from the overarching soul attitude of not-caring, not-loving.

MM: You also see that all the things with which we've afflicted ourselves we've projected onto the honeybee.

GH: Exactly.

MM: Just think of how many chemicals, agents, medicines—toxic types of medicine—infiltrate our own bodies, our own culture, and how we think we can't live without them. And so we think the bees can't live without them. I'm sure you've heard this before, but so many conventional beekeepers get pretty angry and defensive about not using chemicals in the care—I would not even call it care—of honeybees.

GH: As the bees represent the best in us, it is clear that it is exactly that which is severely under attack. Steiner says that the honeybees are so advanced in their being as a group soul that they're not adjusted to the current social conditions. The social conditions two hundred years ago were actually better than now in some respects. At least people who worked hard could provide a living for their families. Now we have people working three jobs who are still not able to provide sustenance for their family.

MM: And the bees were much healthier, too.

GH: Yes. But bees were kept on every farm, by the monks and some teachers. Up to the last third of the 19th century there were no professional beekeepers in the modern sense. And these naturally have to make a living. And to make a living all kinds of things are invented that help mechanize natural processes, that make beekeeping easier and more profitable. The negative side effects, as with most modern medicines, are seen further down the road.

MM: Indeed. So how do we return to the garden?

GH: I'm reminded of the Paradise Play that we performed at the Waldorf Schools in Germany. When Adam and Eve get kicked out of that beautiful garden of paradise, they say, "Well, can't we ever come back?" The angel Gabriel with the fiery sword says, "We will call you back, bit by bit." So, through a lot of work, an enormous amount of inner and outer work, we will come back, but with a transformed consciousness that will be the fruit of developing, in freedom, our higher Self and transforming the Earth into a planet of Love. And the main thing is actually (which ties into our Michaelic Age right now) the spiritualization of the understanding of Nature, of the human being, of evolution—a spiritual understanding that will complement, not eliminate, the materialistic understanding. Without that, we will not make it. I'm positive about that. That is the task of first order. The other one is to go out to and respect all nations, all races, all creeds; to overcome nationality and to overcome the dominant importance of our blood ties. Not that we shouldn't love our relatives, but we may find a sister in Japan or somewhere in Africa. There is such an antiforce worldwide with all the nationalistic movements at this time. And to be brotherly is the third important task in our times. If someone is freezing and I have an extra coat... what do I do? Or if I'm a banker and I get $42 million in salary... the greed is nearly unbelievable. The three main tasks are actually presented in the ideals of the French and American Revolutions: liberty, equality, fraternity. Meaning: in the spiritual and cultural realm, that is, regarding that which we believe in, we should be free. In our being human, regardless of nationality, religion or race we should be equal under the law. And in our daily needs—since we all eat, drink, need clothing and a shelter—we should be brotherly. In all three realms we are under the threat of losing the progress we have achieved over the last few centuries, and those ideals are being replaced with idols. Yes, there is another, a better, America still alive in the dreams of many individuals.

And it's the honeybees—not the frogs or bats, or thousands of insect and bird species also suffering—it's the honeybees that are trying so hard to wake us up to the need to change our ways, to use the crisis as a real opportunity to find again the path that will lead us into the future we are meant to evolve toward.

PEACEFUL WATERS

Katie Hartsock

i.

I stretch out the tongue but tickle his foot
before I put the shoe on. When he's in my arms
and we're laughing, the womb is here, it holds us both.

And we're no closer to leaving the house.
He sticks out his legs, looks to his toes. "They're gardens,"
he says. "My feet are rainy gardens."

ii.

Deinos is a very good Greek word,
it means awful and awesome at once, like awesome itself used to mean
awful and awesome at once. Either way, step back.

This is the child whose eyes I watch fill
with what genuinely looks to be a fratricidal urge
as he pushes down the baby, my baby just learning to walk.

And what furies howl within me, who would tear down and
knock out anyone who hurt my baby's tender limbs braving the hardwood
floors. His confused face as he lands on his back.

Anyone except this one,
with dimpled knees and a smear of blackberry jam dried on his cheek
as he stands over his fallen brother.

In the *Iliad* a goddess says, "Beware,
child, lest I hate you as much as I now terribly love you."
The "terribly" there is the adverbial form of *deinos*.

iii.
We go wading in the river,
shadows and sunlight gleaming on its surfaces. "I can see time,"
he says. "What?" I say. "Time, mama. I can see time." He nods.

iv.
Not long after this I start listening, obsessively,
to John Prine's "Lake Marie." Go now, you, look it up and play it loud.
I listen to it so much I forget

to turn it off when I have him in the car with me—
the song sings the scene of a double murder,
and "faces horribly disfigured by some sharp object."

v.
Later that day we are rolling walnuts down the sidewalk,
the essence of the green-carpeted shells
leaving a scent so crisp on my hands I can taste it.

"I've been standing by peaceful waters today," he said:
a variation on the refrain of the song.
Have you listened to it yet? Good.

Then you know we can carry all the love in the world wherever we go
but violence will have arrived ahead of us
and taken the best bed for itself.

I turn it up on warm autumn days, I shout
"shadows—*shadows*!!!" out rolled-down windows and it is awesome.
But my boy recognizes the Eden of the refrain,

he recreates its walls and stands outside them, underneath a walnut tree.
Some days the best things are the things he makes up,
and the best I can do is repeat.

THE TREES ARE BENDING THEIR NECKS

John R. P. Russell

The trees are bending their necks
the undergrowth is kneeling
before the buck.
His antlers scrape the undersides of their branches.

The Garden of Wisdom

Andrew Kuiper

ITHIN THE SCRIP-
tural corpus, gar-
dens function at an
architectonic level.
The garden within
the land of Eden is the scene for the
narrative of the Fall and is almost as
much a protagonist as are Adam and
Eve. The Gospels testify that though
the Passion narrative is carried out in
the Upper Room, through the streets
of Jerusalem, and atop Golgotha, it is
in the *garden* of Gethsemane that the
drama of salvation takes place. As St.
Maximus the Confessor so skillfully
articulated, it was among the whisper-
ing olive trees that Christ's human will
was fully perfected in unshakable obe-
dience to the Father—even unto
death. And in the Revelation of John
we see that the end is both like and
unlike the beginning. Unlike Eden,
the site of final communion is
described as a gleaming and bejeweled
temple-city. Yet, flowing from the
heart of the New Jerusalem is a shin-
ing river pouring forth from the
divine throne. And the tree of life
returns, bearing much fruit, with
leaves that are able to heal the nations.
While there are other important *topoi*
in the Scriptures, like deserts, moun-
tains and temples, *the garden* is an
image that insinuates the entire
salvific economy almost by incanta-
tion.

The Septuagint often uses the term
paradise (παράδεισος) to translate
references to the primordial garden of
Eden and the eschatologically restored
garden of Eden (as in Ezekiel). The
New Testament uses the term *paradise*
three times to likewise marry the
image of garden and eschatological
bliss. They are (in order) Christ's
words to the dying thief (Luke 23:43),
Paul's account of his ecstatic vision (2
Corinthians 12:2–4), and in Revelation
to the church of Ephesus (Rev. 2:7). Of
these, it is the Pauline usage that is the
most curious. He speaks specifically of
being taken up into the *third* paradise
or realm of paradise. This should alert
us that the image of a divine garden,
besides having mythological reso-
nances (the garden of the Hesperides
in Greco-Roman tales), would be a
somewhat shared and specific escha-
tological cosmology for first-century
Christians and Jews. Paul did not dis-
card what he was taught among the
Pharisees and at the feet of Gamaliel.
For, as Paul reminds us in the letter to
the Romans, it is to the Hebrew peo-
ple that the oracles of God were given,
and God's gifts and callings are irrevo-
cable.

Unfortunately, apart from some
cryptic references in 2 Enoch, there
simply is no extant material that can
help us reconstruct what that system
was. What we do have, however, are

later rabbinic and Kabbalistic traditions concerning *paradise*—in Hebrew *Pardes* (פרדס)—which are well worth investigating. One of the most enduring rabbinic legends (recounted in the Tosefta and both the Babylonian and Jerusalem Talmud) concerns four sages who enter *Pardes*: Ben Azzai, Ben Zoma, Acher, and Rabbi Akiva. The journey is a perfect example of Rudolf Otto's conception of the holy, for this mystical garden is filled with divine beauty, fascinating and utterly dangerous. The group suffers heavy casualties: Ben Azzai drops dead, Ben Zoma falls into madness, and Acher turns to destructive heresies. It is only Rabbi Akiva who "comes in peace and leaves in peace." The parable was used to demonstrate that secrecy with respect to holy mysteries is not simply due to external threats or profanation but for the sanity and safety of any aspiring hierophant.

During the medieval engagement with Aristotelianism, Maimonides would reinterpret the ascent to *pardes* less as an ecstatic ascent and more as an act of intellectual perception and contemplation. "In Maimonides' *Mishneh Torah*, the intellect of the contemplative who freed his thought of the vanities of this world 'is linked under the seat [of glory] to understand those holy and pure forms'. . . . Interestingly, the contemplation of the forms is equated by Maimonides with 'entering Pardes.'"[1] Though under the influence of Aristotle's relatively naturalistic metaphysics, Maimonides seems to identify these forms with angelic separate intellects and affirms that they are to be found underneath the throne of divine glory.

Another medieval Jewish thinker, Moses de Leon, developed the *pardes* legend in a strikingly different way. Instead of seeing the ascent in purely ecstatic or contemplative terms, he unfolded an understanding of *pardes* as an exegetical journey. Scholem writes that

> Moses de Leon employed this highly suggestive term, so rich in shades of meaning, as a cipher for the four levels of interpretation. Each consonant of the word PaRDeS denotes one of the levels: P stands for *peshat*, the literal meaning, R for *rente*, the allegorical meaning, D for *derasha*, the Talmudic and Haggadic interpretation, S for *sod*, the mystical meaning. The *pardes* into which the four ancient scholars entered thus came to denote speculations concerning the true meaning of the Torah on all four levels. In a work written not much later, Moses de Leon took up this image once again and combined it with the notion of the Torah as a nut composed of shell and kernel.[2]

Patristic and Medieval exegetes also insisted (and perhaps helped inspire) the idea that the truth of Sacred Scripture should be sought with the help of a sophisticated letter/spirit dynamic.

---

[1] Moshe Idel, *Kabbalah: New Perspectives* (New Haven, CT: Yale University Press, 1988), 124.

[2] Gershom Scholem, *On the Kabbalah and Its Symbolism* (New York: Schocken Books, 1965), 57.

Even the recognition of a fourfold mode of reading and the metaphor of the shell and the kernel was a widespread trope. To name one paradigmatic instance, Bernard of Clairvaux when preaching would ardently profess his desire to extract the sweetness "of the Spirit from the barren and tasteless mass of the letter, as I separate grain from chaff, the kernel from its shell, or marrow from the bone."[3]

It is no accident that the Song of Songs was an irresistible text for the masters of spiritual exegesis in both the Jewish and Christian traditions. Nowhere else in the Scriptures is erotic love so manifestly yet enigmatically displayed. The entire drama of the encounter takes place among gardens and gardens within gardens. The *hortus conclusus* and *fons signatus* were always taken among Christians as meaning the Church in her innermost purity. With a delicate but overwhelming associative momentum, this grew in the 12th century into a fertile bower of Marian imagery and even became a site for discussions of fully developed Marian dogma such as the Immaculate Conception. But it was not a quirk of Christianity to see in this text a uniquely powerful feminine reality dwelling in a spiritual paradise. Gershom Scholem describes how the female *Shekhinah* was related to spiritual exegesis and the gardens of Solomon. The *Tikkunei ha-Zohar*

calls the Shekhinah, 'the paradise of the Torah,' *pardes ha-Torah.*

Like Moses de Leon, [it] combines this conception with the motif of the nut: 'The Shekhinah in exile is called pardes [because it is clothed as it were in the four levels of meaning], but itself is the innermost kernel. Accordingly, we also call it nut, and King Solomon said when he entered this Paradise [of mystical speculation]: "I went down into the garden of nuts." '[4]

The spiritual heart of Scripture, however, is not something that can be wrenched open through sheer effort of will or raw intelligence. It is not a code that can be cracked by running the text through a sufficient number of algorithms. Only the pangs of spiritual longing and desire allow the exegete to make her way surefooted along such an immense textual terrain. When someone first begins to suspect that Scripture is itself a vast and productive abyss, a certain semiotic vertigo takes hold. We see this described in Jerome as "an infinite forest of meanings" and by Origen as "a mysterious ocean of divinity or, so to speak, a labyrinth." But the exegete is far from passive in this process, and by the act of interpreting exercises a godlike creativity. Augustine, no exaggerator of human capacities, interpreted the verse "be fruitful and multiply" as an exhortation to constant exegetical production. In virtuoso performance, Augustine reads the verse in an allegorical sense *in order to establish a justification for allegory.* The circularity here is far from vicious and instead provides an insight into a central problem of

---

[3] Bernard of Clairvaux, Sermon 73 on the Song of Songs from *The Life and Works of Saint Bernard*, trans. Samuel J. Eales (John Hodges, 1896), 449.

[4] Scholem, *On the Kabbalah and its Symbolism*, 58 (Song of Songs 6:11).

philosophical hermeneutics. As historical and contingent beings, our readings are always *in media res* and no Archimedean point or foundationalist schema can deliver us from this situation. Augustine already had a taste for what is and is not noble and fitting when he read Genesis. To limit the divine commandment to corporeal reproduction seemed anticlimactic to Augustine, and so he transposed the image of reproduction to the intellectual and interpretive realm. "In this blessing, I recognize that thou hast granted us the faculty and power not only to express what we understand by a single idea in many different ways but also to understand in many ways what we find expressed obscurely in a single statement."[5] It is in keeping with the understanding of the spiritual sense of Scripture as *paradise* that Augustine interprets this polysemy as an Edenic mode of seeing the world and the erotic thirst for truth. We might even hear in this allegory an echo of Diotima's speech to Socrates about how the philosopher desires to join with the eternal forms in the generation of beauty.

But how could there be a spiritual paradise of interpretation before the existence of Sacred Scripture? Emmanuel Falque draws on Hugh of St. Victor and Bonaventure to clarify that Christian hermeneutics is not limited to books written on ink and parchment.

In other words, if there is hermeneutics, it pertains not to texts but to the world, not to words but to life; 'Books are the hearts of men,' says Hugh of Saint Victor, 'and the book of life is the wisdom of God' . . . . Otherwise put, and in order to pass in a new way from phenomenology to medieval philosophy, the experience of the world, in both cases, has primacy over the reading of texts, and the experience of the self has primacy over the conjunction of signs. The proof is the originality of the 'book of the world' (*liber mundi*) over the 'book of Scripture' (*liber Scripturae*) which Bonaventure establishes following Hugh of Saint Victor, and in relation to which only sin justifies a new order of priority; 'It is certain that in the state of innocence man had knowledge of created things and by way of representations he praised, honored and loved God. . . . But when man fell and lost this knowledge, there was no one to lead him back to God. This book, the world, was dead and effaced. Thus another book was necessary by which man was enlightened in order to interpret the metaphors of things. This book is Scripture.'[6]

Humanity in the paradisaical mode reads nature as inscripturated and scripture as conjoined with nature. The two symbol-systems are conjoined and each reveals the depth of the other. No less than Sacred Scripture, we must read nature according to the spirit and not as a dead letter.

---

[5] Augustine, *Confessions* trans. E. B. Pusey (James Parker and Co., 1876), chap. 24.

[6] Emmanuel Falque, *God, the Flesh, and the Other*, trans. Chris Hackett (Evanston, IL: Northwestern University Press, 2014), 14–15.

The garden of Eden, of course, was also a place of holy labor. The Aramaic translation of Genesis even translates the phrase as "to toil in the Law and observe its commandments" and the *Midrash Genesis Rabbah* claims that the dust for Adam was taken from what would become the site of the temple.[7] The pair of Hebrew verbs used in Genesis for "work" and "keep" are closely associated with liturgical service in the temple. The Kabbalistic tradition developed

> an expansion of the biblical account of Paradise: God planted it and he commanded Adam to keep it. Moreover, the ancient description of Jewish esotericism employs the term *Pardes*—a garden—as a designation for esoteric speculations. . . . Kabbalah is thus conceived as the real force maintaining the divine Garden, as Adam was commanded to do by God. This cultivation of the Garden is an ongoing activity.[8]

In his very first work of sophiological speculation, Sergei Bulgakov takes up this theurgic understanding when he calls Adam "the living tool of the divine Sophia."[9] Bulgakov interprets the labor of Adam in the garden and the naming of the animals as part of the cosmic process of perfecting

nature and revealing its sophianicity. Not only is this labor free from exploitation, greed and cruelty, it is a positively artistic and creative activity. In one place he even hints that this art is more properly understood as magic: "in a certain sense one can say that Adam was a white mage before the fall."[10] In a postlapsarian world our task "is to defend and to spread the seeds of life, to resurrect nature."[11] As St. Paul teaches in Romans 8, this resurrection of nature has an irreducibly eschatological *telos*. It cannot dismiss necessity, corruption and evil as illusory, but as things to be overcome through an ongoing process of reconciliation. In other words, in addition to recovering the vision of the world as a *theophany*, we must labor *theurgically* to produce the fullness of God in the world as *all in all*.

What then, does the garden mean for us? Is there a way to reconcile the various meanings of *pardes* and *paradeisos* as ecstatic ascent, philosophical contemplation, mystical exegesis, the *Shekhinah*, Mary, the Church, theurgic labor and eschatological goal? A temptation toward extremes tends to end up annihilating the breadth of approaches indicated by this historical catalogue. The approaches of Spinoza and Jacobi are convenient stand-ins for these types (taken as indicating general characteristics and not detailed analyses). The Spinozist *type* relentlessly pares away idiosyncrasy, history and contingency in order to reveal the divine as everything consid-

---

[7] *Midrash Genesis Rabbah* 14:8 and Gen. 2:15, *Tg. Neofiti* as cited in G. K. Beale's *The Temple and the Church's Mission* (Downer's Grove, IL: InterVarsity Press, 2014).

[8] Moshe Idel, *Kabbalah: New Perspectives*, 183.

[9] Sergei Bulgakov, *The Philosophy of Economy*, trans. Catherine Evtuhov (New Haven, CT: Yale University Press, 2000), 154.

[10] Sergei Bulgakov, *Unfading Light*, trans. Thomas Allan Smith (Grand Rapids, MI: Eerdmans, 2012), 363.

[11] Bulgakov, *The Philosophy of Economy*, 153.

ered in relation to what is infinite, eternal and self-subsistent. Prophecy, liturgy, ecclesiology and dogma are treated with condescension or even as dangerous arenas for general political conflict. The Jacobist *type* falls into an opposite though equally damaging error. In this case, a bare existential decision simultaneously buffers the religious individual from critique at the cost of closing the horizon of metaphysical depth. Through a kind of false humility, this approach elevates faith and theology into a sphere so rarefied that it never touches any systematic human attempt at reflection or the living pulse of nature. The Jacobist ends up admitting that reason and the world are fully explicable on the most reductive terms and is forced to deny the role of understanding and knowledge in deification. Neither of these approaches is adequate to slake the desire for the garden of divine wisdom. The Chalcedonian definition presents us with both the human and divine natures of Christ, indissolubly united and without confusion. This definition, applied appropriately to the human search for wisdom, teaches us that while we distinguish between the divine *exitus* into Creation and the creaturely *reditus* into the Godhead, we should not formally separate these into hermetically sealed spheres of *theology* and *philosophy*. Bulgakov draws out the implications and antinomies of the Chalcedonian definition in this way:

> Is God subject to temporality, do changes occur in him, is anything added to his fullness by the creation of the world and the world process? No, nothing is added, for he is absolute fullness and perfection. But—given this—is divine fullness realized in this world too, is God drawn into the world process with its consummations, times, and season? Yes, for the world is still not completed, and God himself raised the cross and was incarnated for the sake of the world's salvation through a human being.[12]

The path and model for wisdom that wants to see the marriage of nature and spirit, symbol and concept, historicity and eternity, dogma and reflection must take the form of a *poetic metaphysics* or *sapiential theology* which are, in the end, the same thing. This is not a new insight: the theurgic Neoplatonists (Proclus, Iamblichus), many Greek and Latin patristic authors, medieval poet-theologians (Bernard Sylvestris, Alain de Lille), Renaissance Christian Neoplatonists and Kabbalists, several of the English and German Romantics, the 19th-century Catholic Tübingen school, as well as modern Russian Sophiologists, all exemplified different yet consonant forms of this approach. The task at hand is to present a unified vision of these figures while critically sorting through their real differences and developing their projects where deficient or erroneous. Most important of all, though, is the necessity to demonstrate through poetic production the *vivifying* and *fruitful* power contained in this approach which, though in a sense traditional, is ever renewing itself

---

[12] Sergius Bulgakov, *Unfading Light*, 198.

through the dynamic incorporation of fresh insights.

This explains how aspects of *pardes* might be discovered through a lyrical or prophetic rapture (whether the artistic essays of Andrei Belyi or the apostolic journey of St. Paul) without *suppressing* the desire for *pardes* which is expressed in causal analysis, comparison and system building. The wonderful legend of how Francisco Suarez was given metaphysical prowess *by means of appealing to the Virgin Mary*, gives an example of how we should desire to relate the mystical and rhapsodic to more universal and exoteric forms of knowing. More strongly, *without* the enrichment of that mutual exchange, the search for wisdom stalls out into either a stale inventory of dead letters *or* a journey so private and ineffable that it cannot be communicated to the world. Poetry is able to provide a form of knowing that operates on these many levels and maintain cosmic and metaphysical ambitions alongside an intimate spiritual journey. It is no accident that so much of Sacred Scripture is poetry, and a disappointment that the *form* of poetry has not always been recognized as one capable of providing *wisdom* properly speaking.

There are exceptions, of course, like the writings of Bernard Sylvestris and Alain de Lille. But nothing outside of the great religious texts of human history has ever surpassed Dante in *La Vita Nuova* and *The Divine Comedy* in expressing the sapiential dimensions of poetic form. The surpassing role of the feminine in his work reinforces the truth that the garden of *Sophia* will only be found where there is *dialogic eros*. The tears of Beatrice are

what wrench Virgil out of Hell to lead Dante on his way; but, the Virgin Mary, St. Lucy, and the mysterious Matelda are guides and goals in their turn as well. Dante, Statius, and Virgil find Matelda when they reach the peak of the purgatorial mount which is also the garden of Eden in Canto 28 of the *Purgatorio*. She is described by Dante as being graced with prelapsarian innocence. Yet her purity (and by this time Dante is fully purified as well) does not prevent the application of the motif of erotic love from various pagan myths concerning Venus, Proserpina, and Leander. Dante even samples a line from Guido Cavalcanti's *una donna soletta* (an unabashedly sensual pastorella from the greatest of the *Stilnovisti*) and applies it to Matelda in the earthly paradise.

She is brimming with figural significance ranging from that of a nymph (perhaps this should put us in mind of Porphyry's masterwork of Neoplatonist allegory *Cave of the Nymphs*) or even a pagan nature deity to the *vita activa*. She has even been identified as the personification of Wisdom in the Old Testament, and as the exegetical artistry needed to reveal the deep meanings of Scripture and poetry.[13] Matelda herself takes time to honor Statius and Virgil by revealing that whenever the ancient poets sang of Parnassus they were remembering and longing for Eden. Dante clothes Matelda in erotic allusions to argue that innocence is not a privative state. The search for the place where Wis-

[13] See entry "Matelda" in *The Dante Encyclopedia*, ed. Richard Lansing (Philadelphia, PA: Routledge, 2010).

dom dwells calls forth a fury that puts all other expressions of desire to shame.

Both Plato and Pseudo-Dionysius agree that our search for the sapiential garden is primarily the function of *eros*. Far from being an erasure of wonder or an illegitimate grasping for what is transcendent, it is only the longing for divinity which allows us to participate in mysteries that exceed us. And this is a real *chase*, not simply a passive reception or waiting out of *faux* humility. Nicholas of Cusa gives to one of his works the title of *De venatione sapientiae* or *On the hunt for wisdom*. The activity of hunting also appears in *The Ways of Perfect Religion* by St. John Fisher as the paradigm for religious life and he insists that "all true Christian souls be called hunters." St. Bonaventure reminds us that it is only the one who imitates the prophet Daniel in being a *vir desideriorum* who can reach the supernal Jerusalem through the groanings of prayer and the lightning flashes of speculation. The *Zohar* contains a parable of a beautiful woman hidden in a tower who communicates to her lover only by the subtlest and briefest of signs. Because of this, her lover always stands idle in the courtyard attentive for the momentary grace of her appearance. "So it is with the Torah, which discloses her innermost secrets only to them who love her. She knows that whosoever is wise in heart hovers near the gates of her dwelling place day after day. What does she do? From her palace, she shows her face to him, and gives him a signal of love, and forthwith retreats back to her hiding place. Only he alone catches her message, and he is drawn to her with

his whole heart and soul, and with all of his being."[14]

Our desires for wisdom, which are the true depths of each person, could not be satisfied by an *impersonal* object. We want dialogical communion, not depersonalization. The divine persons of the Holy Trinity as well as the communion of saints bear witness to the enduring and essential nature of personal realities in our sapiential hunt. Here, too, we see the power of the feminine figure of *Sophia/Hokhmah* in the Wisdom books of the Old Testament. In Proverbs 8 we learn that Wisdom was possessed by the Lord in the beginning of His ways and her constant rejoicing is His delight. In Sirach 24 Wisdom exults that she has come forth from the mouth of the Most High as first among creatures and the one who fills men with understanding like "a water channel into a garden." And, most explicitly, the seventh chapter of the Wisdom of Solomon says, "She is a breath of the power of God/and a pure emanation of the glory of the Almighty" and "a reflection of the eternal light/a spotless mirror of the working of God." The entire cosmos, in its structure, life, being, and receptivity to divinity, must be understood in at least partially personal terms, or as Bulgakov puts it, "enhypostatically." The Mother of God, of course, is the fullest personal realization of *Sophia* as the response of the soul of Creation to the Creator. This is acknowledged in the divine liturgy by the reading of Proverbs 8 assigned to the feast of the Immaculate Conception in the *usus*

---

[14] *The Zohar*, "The Lovers of the Torah," trans. Scholem (New York: Schocken, 1995).

antiquior of the Tridentine rite. As St. Bernadette insisted to her local priest, Mary is not simply *immaculately conceived* she is *the Immaculate Conception* itself: a dogma which Vladimir Solovyov recognized as a perfect confirmation of his own sophiological writings. It is fitting (if not outright providential) that *sapientia, sophia*, and *hokhmah* are all feminine nouns, as they train our imaginations to look for a female presence that embodies wisdom.

The Marian valence of the sapiential books of the Old Testament did not go unnoticed during the High Middle Ages. The French canon Richard of Saint Laurent unabashedly uses such phrases as "Mary, that is to say, Wisdom" and "the words of Wisdom are the words of Mary." By containing the fiery word of God in her womb, she also became in some way deified and the possessor of all wisdom and knowledge. In his *De laudibus beatae Mariae Virginis*, Richard systematically applied the names, symbols, and figures of the sapiential books to Mary. "If, however, anyone should judge me rash in assembling such concordances, he ought to know, that truly whatever the ancients said concerning divine Wisdom, the moderns expound concerning the mother of Wisdom for whom with Wisdom so intricate is the union, that while her generation may be univocal, she is called Wisdom by equivocation."[15] In Kabbalah, this presence particularly united to the Godhead is known as the *Shekhinah* and it has been argued that its formulation in medieval Jewish mysticism owes no small part to Marian piety and theology.[16]

Both traditions insist that God dwells with us (in the tabernacle, temple, or Incarnation) through a nuptial relationship with a female figure who guides us into the heart of revelation and creation. Mary, besides being singled out as one with deep meditative insight into the divine economy in the Gospel of Luke (2:19, 51), was also attributed with skill in all kinds of wisdom, including exegesis of sacred scripture and metaphysics. This may be a corollary of the belief that Adam and Eve in their paradisaical state had superior gifts of contemplation and metaphysical insight that were lost after the Fall. Mary was considered to be not only the New Eve but (via Irenaeus) the new *garden of Eden*. Irenaeus boldly pairs the creation of Adam from the dust of the incorrupt garden with the flesh of Christ being produced from the virgin flesh of Mary! Combining these images produces a vision of Mary as a living symbol of both the unfallen cosmos *and* the perfect ability to perceive and interpret that cosmos. She returns to that state of which Bonaventure said no Scripture was needed to read the metaphors of nature. But instead of jettisoning the history of revelation

---

[15] See pp. 251–308 on Richard of Saint Laurent in Rachel Fulton Brown's *Mary and the Art of Prayer* (New York: Columbia University Press, 2019).

[16] See Arthur Green, "Shekinah, the Virgin Mary, and the Song of Songs: Reflections on a Kabbalistic Symbol in its Historical Context" and *Keter: The Crown of God in Early Jewish Mysticism* (Princeton: Princeton University Press, 2016); also P. Schafer, *Mirror of His Beauty: Feminine Images of God from the Bible to the Early Kabbalah* (Princeton: Princeton University Press, 2002).

and its artifacts, Mary sits at the heart of the world and helps draw us through the meanings of nature, Scripture, and tradition to her son the God-Man who is *the* image and word of the Father. In this way she becomes a new paradise. As Abbot Eckbert said, "Truly you are the paradise of God, who gave to the world the tree of life, from which whoever eats shall have eternal life.... And you are more than a paradise: for he who drinks water from it will thirst again. O how much you gave to the world, who merited to be the aqueduct of such healing waters!"[17]

Mary combines the roles of Diotima and Ariadne in helping us to enter into the sacred mysteries and leading us through the complicated texts and symbols that make up the multiplicity of this world in the process of reconciliation. She is all the Hesperidean nymphs dancing together guarding the garden of golden apples and unafraid of the hundred-headed dragon. It is in these very roles of guard, guide, and mystagogue that the 16th-century cardinal and head of the Augustinian order Giles of Viterbo *explicitly identifies* the Virgin Mary, Mother of God, with the Kabbalistic *Shekhinah*. Daniel Stein-Kokin relates how Giles received a beautiful Hebrew codex of the Pentateuch (and some additional texts) from Pope Leo X. Within that codex is an image of the city of Jericho as a massive labyrinth and the house of Rahab. Stein-Kokin points out that not only does this demonstrate that the mythic image of the labyrinth was *not* missing from or avoided by Jewish and Christian mystics but it is also a likely source of inspiration for the structure of Giles of Viterbo's late work on the Shekhinah. In this work Giles, writing in the first person *as the Shekhinah,*

> likens the mysteries, which this feminine emanation of the Godhead (according to the Kabbalah) has stored away, to 'circuitous sacred oracles,' to 'a labyrinth of writings' 'inaccessible to mortals' and to which 'there is no hope of [entry] ... unless with the thread of Rahab extended from the window.' Egidio's Shekinah proceeds to identify this thread as her own way of proceeding, adding that 'faith ... offers to the wise a thread.' On another occasion, Egidio again refers to the thread of Rahab in the context of 'the enigmas and intricate windings of the divine labyrinth.' And here the Shekinah reveals that she 'gave this thread, this pattern, this model to the apostles' in the hope that, their minds having been filled with the Holy Spirit and the sefirot (we later learn that these are the means by which miracles are performed), 'their lines and thread will be extended throughout the whole world.'[18]

Lastly, wisdom is not only a matter of contemplation but of divine power to transfigure the world. We see this power most purely when bread and wine become the flesh and blood of

---

[17] Rachel Fulton Brown, *Mary and the Art of Prayer*, 298.

[18] Daniel Stein-Kokin, "Entering the Labyrinth: On the Hebraic and Kabbalistic Universe of Egidio Da Viterbo."

divinity; yet, we must remember that the entire range of creative and productive human energy are meant to be consecrated. Creation is brought toward its Creator and, no less powerfully, the Creator is brought into his Creation. Like an illuminated manuscript, teeming with plant and animal life, fairies and monsters, the symbols and dynamism of nature must fully inhabit the word of God and make sure that we never reduce the divine to merely verbal or propositional content. Friedrich Oetinger, Pietist Lutheran, expressed a similar desire never to expound Scripture without taking stock of the works of God. In his *Small Confession* he declares that "in holy things there must be a harmony of all—in nature also." Or as Friedrich Schlegel eloquently puts it:

> the loving soul is the clear mirror in which we gaze upon the secrets of divine love either reflected or symbolically figured as so many enigmas . . . we plainly behold the ever-verdant and immortal plants or hidden flowers of nature, like the dark bed of the deep through the clear waters of a still sea.[19]

We will not be able to peer through the iron cage of nature's necessity or a static and desiccated liberalism in Scripture without discerning the New Paradise as the heart of each. And we will not have the power to join in holy labor to build up this vision of paradise without the love for Wisdom herself and an acceptance of her motherly care and rule in the spiritual *ecclesia* on earth.

[19] Friedrich Schlegel, *Lectures on the Philosophy of Language,* trans. Rev. A. J. W. Morrison (New York: Harper and Brothers, 1848), Lecture 1.

FOUR POEMS

R. Bratten Weiss

ONE MORNING IN SUMMER

In the morning in my garden I find that instead of vegetables I have planted
     cities.
The buildings are about knee-high, like corn in July.
The bells in the tiny church are the size of my fist, and they're all ringing,
because a giant has come, striding towards them through the clover.
Terrified white faces under pointed hats peer out of windows.
Miniscule mothers grab babies and rush into doorways.

I remember how Gulliver felt, on his travels, but Gulliver discovered his
     tiny cities—
he didn't plant them. They were not his responsibility.

If the people huddled in fright gazing up at me, a few with antique
     blunderbusses
long as my thumb, think me a cannibal, why shouldn't they?
I planted this garden with every intention of eating what it grew.

I ought to be astonished at what I have done. I always wanted whole empires
didn't I? Adoring subjects to kneel before me? But at the moment I am mostly
Annoyed. I didn't want cities, I didn't want subjects, I wanted only tomatoes.
Tomatoes red and yellow and purple, tomatoes like golden orbs, tomatoes like
     rubies,
tomatoes like an enemy's skull, dripping sweet juice, seeds bursting as I bite
     down.

Here I stand a Titan, and a tiny beautiful warrior is rushing at me
with his tiny glittering sword unsheathed, and I am full of awe,
I am proud of these my people, so bold and reckless.

It is hopeless for the tiny warrior to take me on, it is all
hopeless, we keep on getting cities when we asked for gardens,
our skulls are soft as fruit, our fists are helpless, and maybe now
there will never be tomatoes again.

SPANCEL

It will only work at night, in the rain, and only in spring
when the dying of things is less visible. You will want
to wait until all the others are asleep, so they don't see
you creeping out naked as a needle under your oilskins,
so they don't ask you, hey mom, where are you off to
with that knife, mom, can I have some crackers, mom,
can I watch Star Wars, who wrote The Trumpet of the Swan?

In the dark the rain will be thick like ghosts trying to get
their fingers on your skin, the flowers will open their tiny
white mouths and sing of all the forbidden things you want
to keep on wanting, and the grass is rich with an orgy of
earthworms making baby earthworms and shitting soil.

If you're serious about this, what you need to do is cut
three branches each of dogwood, lilac, and wild apple.
Then very carefully peel away the skin, peeling it in coils
tiny as thread. We used to skin bodies for this, by the way,
but that isn't very nice, and is frowned on by the Better
People, so now we use branches. The trees don't seem to care.

Now, you take the ribbons of bark, loop them together,
make a lariat. Whatever you throw it over, it's yours.
not just things, either. Find a man sleeping, coil him in bark,
he'll never get over you. You could have a passion wild as the
earthworms. You really could. Or you could just pass through,
listen to the singing. Try destroying nothing, for a change.

WEEDING

I am suspended in a fist, roots helpless,
everything drying, a feast deep in dark
now is gone, guests gone worms curling
blindly, hurt by light. My mouths open close
open close open on nothing.
Dirt falls like rain.

Hard nails tear at hard soil,
soil breaks, nails break, roots break
sweat streaks dirt on arms.

When the Jamestown settlers discovered a new plant in the new world
they thought they could make a salad of it, but the plant was toxic.
They fell mad, and gibbered like monkeys. "Jamestown weed" they named
it—Jimson weed, today.

At no point have I looked at Jimson weed and thought "A salad!" But then
I have never thought things were there for my taking. You have to wonder
what those colonists were thinking, that they could eat these leaves and nothing
would turn around and attack their brains.

If the weed in my hand had teeth, would turn and bite me?

When cabbages are attacked by cabbage moth larvae they emit a scent that
attracts a parasitic wasp that lays its eggs on the larva. When the eggs hatch
The wasp larvae suck the moth larva dead from the inside out. You can encourage
these wasps to hang around, if you plant companion crops, like dill between the
cabbages.

Any of us with our roots under mulch come up easy.
We were not expecting this.
She is throwing us over her shoulder, she is piling us high.
We were separate once, but now we die together.

Pigweed
lamb's quarters
plantain
purslane
wild carrot
Queen Anne's lace
creeping charlie
jimson weed.
Everything is its own burial mound.

NIGHT PERSON

The starlings kept eating all the breadcrumbs and the
cats kept running off with the chunks of meat so finally
I settled on baiting the front lawn just with pieces of bone.
In the moonlight the ribs curved neatly round the skulls
like some long sinuous creature had settled for its winter
nap before the snows came, before the wind took its flesh.

I wait now under the dogwood tree, folded in a square of
dark, thinking, I don't have much time, I hope it comes
soon. Otherwise I'd have to put all the bones away before
morning, or try to fabricate excuses. Like, what, the bones
on the lawn? No worries, it's a new kind of landscaping.
Or, the bones are good for the plants. And yes I put them
out at night, I'm a night person, aren't I?

But it's okay, the great winged creature is coming, its
breath like hot gold, and it stoops to where I sit in my
little origami fold of darkness, and I rise to greet it.
My joints crack like dry wood. The night was long.

Seating myself fragile on its leather back, I see my hands
have become pale mottled claws clutching its black spines.
My hair is a white snarl. The creature bends its neck and
looks at me with flaming eyes, speculative, like this wasn't
the queen he'd come looking for.

What can I tell him? That it isn't my fault? That something
else had entered the circle of bones, something hungry? When
I wasn't looking it must have plucked and pecked away at
everything I'd hoarded there.

I'm not passing up this chance, now that my dragon has
arrived, but there's a good chance I'll fall, and it won't be
like Icarus.

You may find me, another old rib, fertilizing the lawn.

TWO POEMS

Rick Yoder

TRIPTYCH OF EDEN

In this house, this pharos
where the waves break slow
under the dancing bridge
and the bridgehead beached in flesh
like a hook in the heart of my mouth
splitting the spirals of my longing
lips tight-racked open where the foam
runs thick and straight.
Not like me; like my shadow.
The keys turn slow like grasshoppers
before the zephyr. And I, before the plow.

The wizened paint unwhitened by the sun,
we thought it would be, expected to find
a wraith or glass the color of forgetting.
And the open wind, wound of the sky
jutting forth in the table's middle place
where a candle flickers, unheld.
The loose flame cannot remember
a time before oxygen. We cannot
peer beyond the gate of dawn.

Before I go to the brindled place,
bridled like your hand inside his glove,
before I go, as broken as the rib
when you were carried off upon the path
with only one beginning, before I go,
and just one end to speak of – mine alone,
out of this shadow-garden, into shade,
into the orchard of remembering. Before I go,
this bone, this flute, this road upon the bridge
bleeds from out my father's reddened side,
light pouring from the house of my return.

BOSQUET

Face fixed into a marble mask and hide
where the grove shudders still and grows
more like an absence, more like rain
that captures itself in a whistling flume
riddle of gold hidden in its lusty vein
dash of the sun, peacock in his pride
and every other fit of lesser glory
mounted to his quiet marble wall.

BERRY PICKING

Paul Hunter

Between city and cemetery,
On the Troy bike trail,
We gathered black raspberries grown wild.
Each one is an upturned chalice,
Ready to spill its blood dark juices.
Son and daughter,
your hands and cheeks stained deep purple,
Sunshine and breezes braided in our hair,
We tumbled down the hillside,
Lay in the drowsy grass,
Overlooking our city.
For your Father,
And for all who live under the moon,
Here is all eternity.

The World as Garden

Scot F. Martin

> "I want to awake in you a deep admiration for creation, until you in every place, contemplating plants and flowers, are overcome by a living remembrance of the creator."— St. Basil

ARRIVED HOME FROM Christmas at my in-laws to an email message informing me of beavers in my nearby park. Understand that I live in a hub suburb of Detroit. Beavers (*Castor canadensis*) were extirpated in SE Michigan during the middle of the American Civil War. They have since made a reappearance in the Detroit River recently (which isn't really a river, it's a strait). The Upper Rouge River (which *is* a river), one of four branches, meanders through my neighborhood. That spills into the Detroit River, and the Rouge is where beavers are now sporadically sighted.

The Rouge, along with three other American urban rivers, has the distinction of catching fire—yes, the rivers burned—back in the late 60's and early 70's. That horrific scene of a 50-foot high wall of flame consuming the industrial waste on the water's surface helped to spur the Clean Water Act of 1972.

So, after I unpacked the presents and gear, I headed over to the park with my camera, a short two-minute jaunt from doorway to riverbank. Sure enough, I found evidence of the visit. Some young cottonwoods had been felled, others partially gnawed on. The scene was reminiscent of teen-aged vandalism. No lodge had been constructed; this didn't appear to be anything other than a snack bar for the rodents. Perhaps they were building upstream or down. Still… beavers in my neighborhood. When we treat the land, water, and air like God commands, good things happen—like beavers in my neighborhood.

❖ ❖ ❖

However one wishes to take the primordial origin story of mankind, we all read that it has its genesis in a garden. This is different from a wilderness, which in imaginations as recent as the Puritans in colonial New England saw that space as a vector of chaos, teeming with wild, man-eating animals, barbarians, cannibals, and demonic forces beyond the ken of human knowledge or control.

A garden is a safe space, relatively speaking, that can provide contemplation, re-creation, food, or beauty; sometimes all of that together. The providence of a God who is love would place the progenitors of humanity in such a space and not a wilderness; a place of serenity and provision, not a landscape where hunter-gatherers eke out survival.

What do we do with a garden, but cultivate it? What does it mean to cultivate?

The *Concise OED* traces the word from Medieval Latin—two words meaning land and inhabit, and of course, it's related to culture. We don't think of inhabiting a garden today, but what would happen if we envisioned the world entire as a garden and all creatures as features of that garden?

If we thought about and practiced cultivation in all areas of our lives what would that look like? Friends and family, employers and employees, strangers, even. What is the soil, water, and sunlight for these relationships?

Henry Ford completed the Rouge plant in 1928 as the largest integrated plant in the world at the time. The plant still operates to this day (churning out Ford F-150 trucks), located near the mouth of the Rouge River. The river served as a convenient place to dump waste for Ford. Other plants located near the Rouge complex followed the practice of dumping into the water as well. So, in 1969, some stray sparks from an acetylene torch ignited the chemicals and solid waste that formed an ersatz floating crust on the Rouge. Several companies of fire stations were called to kill the conflagration.

The care of a garden begins with the soil. From there one plants in a place designed to get the right amount of sunlight; one waters and weeds, and if all has gone right, one harvests. The rest is a mystery.

We can follow a similar pattern for relationships. We spend time, money, we reveal our inner selves (depending on the relationship, of course), we commiserate and empathize; the rest is a mystery.

What do we do in the natural world? If we follow the suburban model: mow, poison, and pave. But if we viewed our neighborhood as a garden, perhaps we would remember who originally planted the oaks, birches, maples, and pines. Perhaps we might more carefully consider our actions there.

Who gave the bison the urge to roam and graze? The red squirrel the acrobatic training and desire to chatter and scold? Who designed the bluegill to float in the water column waiting for food? Certainly not us.

We may have lost the original garden, but does that mean everywhere else east, north, south, and west of Eden is open for rapacious extraction, plowing, annihilation, and despoiling? Most likely in your neighborhood whatever remains of pre-settlement topography and vegetation suffers from ignorance and neglect.

I have tried my hand at vegetable gardening with some limited success—my cilantro always bolted before I could harvest it—and I'm most proud of the time I harvested arugula in December, but I made the switch to native forbs and grasses in my yard. Why? For me, ecology is easier, and more pleasurable than agriculture. I could cite some high-minded reasons from entomologist Doug Tallamy and other ecologists hurrahing the value of native plants in our yards. I recognize that gardening or farming with the Lordship of Christ in mind should bring in beneficial creatures, but rather than worrying about the pests and if I'll be able to harvest those sugar-snap peas, I prefer to enjoy a parade of pollinators on my plants and the insectivores that hang around the shagbark hickory.

The potent explosion of orange in July when the butterfly weed blooms, or the threatening blue-green texture of rattlesnake master, and the late spring splash of deep purple spiderwort blossoms all bring a different kind of joy to me than tomatoes, potatoes, or corn. Knowing that I'm creating a small food plot for others is a way to love my neighbors. Of course, these neighbors aren't human, but that is irrelevant.

Would you like an easy way to love your neighbor? Learn their names. Whether it's Jack or Sheena, Marquise or Racine, José or Carol, or even something a bit harder like *Marmota monax*, *Anax junius*, or even *Acer nigrum*, learning his or her name is the first step in getting to know someone—from there perhaps that relationship will bloom into love.

Screech owls, Baltimore orioles, and peregrine falcons have all been through my back yard, the orioles wove a nest in the American beech (*Fagus grandifolia*) that watches over my home. Toads, groundhogs, and damselflies all have found food on the small piece of earth I lay claim to. Granted, the usual species that are cozy with humans live near me, too: skunk, raccoon, opossum, house sparrow, gray and fox squirrel, and many others. The less common visitors are the ones that direct my thoughts to the Father in gratitude for a moment or two of grace.

The Rouge River hasn't healed itself—there is still much work to accomplish. One lover of the river I know calls it "a broken river for a broken-hearted people," but successful restoration has begun. Whereas annual cleanups consisted of pulling rusted-out cars and abandoned boats from the river now the "rescues" concentrate on controlling invasive plant species or even sowing native plants to participate in the redemption of the earth.

Jesus initiated a relationship with me when I was thirteen. The church that nourished me until I was about 20 subtly preached quite a bit of anti-ecology (along the lines of "It's all going to burn, so why should we put effort into restoring the world?"). I hear less and less of that, perhaps because Catholics don't usually think that way. What I do hear increasing is a default anti-human "Deep Ecology," especially on social media. "I hate people—look at what they've done to the land, water, species X. I wish they'd all die."

Both positions are wrong for anyone willing to spend some time in scripture and to follow the traditions handed down from the fathers and mothers of the church. We hybrid beings (flesh and spirit) are meant to be regents of creation (read C.S. Lewis' Narnia series for another take on that). The world can heal, perhaps not completely, but the effort is worth it. If we treat the world as a garden that needs to be nurtured, we will soon discover wonder and mystery, and, perhaps, that the beavers have stopped by our neighborhood for a bite or twelve of cottonwood.

MATINS

Tom Sturch

for my sons

A dark star, perhaps a bird in daylight hours,
fell through the maze of the garden canopy.

This is to report that some visitations may undo us,
that being is contingent, but that with practice
the eye will deepen to receive eccentric kinds of light.
This is to say how the residue of sleep
can make it hard to sort wing from wing
when the shards of the daybreak sky
appear as both silhouettes in the trees and
the crazing, apocalyptic dome,
when night after night
the garden enlarges her borders with waiting, aroma and mist,
winding the hours with invitation and angels.

As for my dark visitor, I admit an immediate instinct to flight—
to resort indoors to figure the stranger out—
to solve between the avian and angelic.

I feel I must explain: this event falls on the heels of
other god-like appearances—
raccoon and hawk, possum and heron—surprising from the garden cover
to expose me as irrational, visceral, comical…

But this morning came the stark unknown.
And as I stood in the pale yellow cone of the porch light
dropping seed for the early wrens,
I wondered if the sound of grain on the pebbles and weeds at my feet
held the measure of what being it would be.

✛ ✛ ✛ ✛ ✛ ✛

One might think this an affectation. But being is never
not real. Truth is, I relish in the hour's enigma—
the Night Garden classroom

that challenges the black and white of day—
the press of body into soul that human knowing is:
the apparent paradox of light from darkness,

anticipation as prolonged state,
the impossible graduation of color at the edge of perception,
the range from intimacy to industry

the child to glory is. And for things of the dawn
that manifest without founding:
the working out of faith in simple immersion,

or casting the spell of praise from despair—
listening, compounding in a rosette of years
until the whispers of nature console without words.

Sitting in witness on the night's finishing hours—
as figments feel for the great oak's recesses,
lights retrieve their empty nets,

and stars retire without solving all the night's fears.
To encounter the creatures who invite us to labors
with all the world drenched in blue.

✤ ✤ ✤ ✤ ✤ ✤

I recall, once, early in the hour, a reverie:

I imagined the tessellated dome as hungry seabirds on the
wharf awaiting the always-arriving lover of the earth—the sun

inbound for the widening berth of the garden's ocean sky.
That his ship of light home from exotic ports rode low

in its hold of alexandrite and pink ivory, the wind in sails of gold.
And the garden awaited her glory knowing these adventures

are a sublimate for his ceaseless burning. Then,
he kissed her dew-filled bower with fire

and proved that on this
as with each day of splendor,

he is hers.

✤ ✤ ✤ ✤ ✤ ✤

All of this compels me to wonder
how it is we are not crushed with wonder—

how shadow remains possible
given the little attention we pay to light—

how even the sun finds its form
erupting against the gravity of its being

and how the pirouetting earth
turns her face so quickly

to the brilliance of the light's immolation.
And as the tumbling bowl of night

returns each day I wonder how it is we
survive the angels—

so needful are we of darkest sleep—
how they bear with us

in our abuse of the light and stay with us
in our need of it—

how they keep silent watch in sleepless hours.
I want you to know

that we are not the light, but its children—
mere seed in need of the angel's

help to die. Not as a curse as some
would think, but awakening

to a daily inheritance of labors
as tenders of new life.

✣ ✣ ✣ ✣ ✣ ✣

A confession: after years of life's proving I now
believe the poet's *dying of the light*
makes too much philosophy of nostalgia.

It was the Icarus in us that made us *thus to rage.*
And I want to say I have learned
to return my failures, thankfully, to the ground

and humbly extend my worn and useless wings to
the Athenas and sires, prodigals in the world,
who spend their time listening to the air

for something new—unaware that we raised them on
fantasies of flight—their joy in the earth now a casualty
of their wars against irony—

their unanswered questions of paternity—
out of which mind they flew—
in the days we labored without hearts.

I desire that they would return to find us
on sullied knees, burying our degrees
like *memento mori,* with better hopes of rooting

into the corporeal genius of the world—
where even our dying, like certain science,
becomes a task at which *no one ever does more*

than not utterly fail.
That the light and its children find us
laden with fruit and praising.

✢ ✢ ✢ ✢ ✢ ✢

And here at last is the sun; the bird, red as dawn
has eaten and flown. So, today's work begun
we'll gather tomorrow, gardens apart,
children of light in the vanishing dark
to treasure the till of our human soil
as fruitful enrichment, turning mind with soul.
And take care, dark to light, to deepen our seeing,
take courage when facing our angels of being;
reap joy raining down in the rising songs;
and tend birds of the air on the ground of the sun's revelations.

Gardens: Sites of Resistance

Darrell Lackey

HEREVER WE FIND any meta or cosmic resistance to the, as St. Paul put it, rulers, authorities, the cosmic and spiritual powers—the principalities (Eph 6:12), we find gardens. Rather than the building of forts, the clenching of teeth, or the stoking of fires, we find the cultivation of flowers, bushes, trees, grass, and vines—we find beauty, peace, solace and food. Any reflection of a raised fist here is but the morning dew on a blade of grass.

What could possibly be subversive about a garden? What could roses presume to resist? What power is conveyed, what fear in one's enemies is struck, by flashes of dancing colored petals, lush green labyrinths, vines dripping with grapes, bushes, and trees teaming with life? What could tender reeds, easily bruised and bent, signal to any archon powers? It seems preposterous.

Gardens, whether material or mythic, physical or trope, are repeated images and locations in the Christian narrative. Another is the city. The city is presented in the Bible as the site of hubris, violence, and vice (Babylon), but also as the earthly throne of God (Jerusalem). Graham Ward writes:

The Bible is ambivalent towards cities. The first cities were built by men of demonstrable power and ambition. Cain, having murdered his brother Abel and being informed by God that he would be a vagabond all his life, 'built a city, and called the name of the city after the name of his son, Enoch' (Genesis 4:17). The origins of the city, for the Bible, seem to lie in masculine expressions of defiance, insecurity, the need to find substitutions and consolations for the loss of God.[1]

However, the garden in the biblical narrative remains not so ambivalent. It is something unspoiled and pure, even if a death occurred there; well, all deaths occurred there. The spiritual death of man in the garden leads to Abel's physical death and thus, the building of cities. While cities seemed to be marked in the same way as Cain, gardens arise from the prophetic soil that cries out to God as it accepts the blood of Abel.

The garden is also elusive. It is somehow not only as real as the dirt beneath our feet, but as untouchable as Eden. Living East of there, the echo

---

[1] Graham Ward, *Cities of God* (London: Routledge, 2000), 32.

of Woodstock is not only a vibration centered in a specific time and place, but Joni Mitchell picks up on something that has echoed down the ages—to wit: We need to get back to the garden. Somehow if we can retrace our steps, get back to where it began, we will be at peace again. The garden is all at once hope and resolution, but something like Wolfe's home as well—the place to which we can never return.

The garden is here, but not yet. It is eschatological. It is apocalyptic. The garden is many things, but I say again, it is the place of resistance. It is a place of warfare, only of a different type. It is the prophetic announcement and forensic location of both heaven and hell. It is where both serpent and God walk amongst us. It is unspoiled and pure yet witness to the most terrible of events. For here, among other more sublime moments, mankind fell, and Jesus pled for cups to pass.

In the Garden of Eden, we see the first resistance to the principalities and powers. Here knowledge was not gained, only the ability to mistake knowledge, or wisdom, for making judgments—for deciding between right and wrong. Noticing one is naked and making a negative judgment about such is not knowledge or wisdom. It is to mistake an observation for an ethical judgment and, worse, as ours to make. Such was to slander the truth that creation was good. In not allowing this to be considered truthful, the garden becomes the very place of resistance to the idea that the principalities and powers can tell us what is true about creation— about ourselves. The coverings for sin were made here, in the garden. And it

was here in the garden where a death sentence and declaration of war were announced against the serpent and any powers associated with the fallen angel.

In the Garden of Gethsemane, we see the next significant resistance to the principalities and powers. Again, in a garden takes place events of cosmic proportion. In this idyllic setting, there are encounters, struggles, both against the flesh and those who represent the violence of the rulers and powers. Jesus faces the terrible truth of the path before him. A path made necessary by events in another garden. In St. Luke's account, Jesus is in great anguish. Here angels attend. Not on some wide plain, or desolate field where great armies gather, but here in a garden does a battle take place that would far dwarf even the most horrible collision of all the armies of the world.

If all heaven and hell are watching now, we could only imagine a chilling gasp of air, fearful of even taking another breath. What battlefield, what zones or corridors of resistance have ever witnessed such a gargantuan upheaval of categories up to this moment (God in anguish, God seized by men)—and all in a garden? The inward struggle of will and flesh, the outward appearance of the "chief priests, the officers of the temple police, and the elders" (Matt 22:52), bring together the twin engines the principalities and powers use to wage war against the inhabitants of gardens and life.

Did Adam do the same in his instance? Do *we* (we are Adam)? Is this what love and resistance looks like? Or is it only here that the struggle, the fight, the battle, took place? In the first instance, Adam, under the cover of blood, escapes East. Here, in this garden, there is no escape. But escape was never an option. Here, soft grass met rough boots and leaves, scrubby beards. God, the Alpha and Omega, the Beginning and the End, is led away by men. Swords and men of violence mimic the "sword flaming and turning to guard the way to the tree of life…" as they drive the second man from this garden.

There is a remaining garden, however. Like the previous ones, this one too is a place of resistance and spiritual warfare. In each, despite the assault of events, God doesn't allow the powers to have the last word, even though it might appear they lay great waste to the halcyon serenity of these sites, these spaces. We see death, anguish, and violence even here. But we also see a resistance, a different type of warfare, and one wonders if the setting, a garden, is the first hint, our first clue, that their very being is a strategic reminder or nod toward life, creation, beauty, abundance, and victory.

In St. John's Gospel (19:41), we read of our third garden: "Now in the place where he was crucified there was a garden, and in the garden a new tomb in which no one had yet been laid." Was it lost on the principalities and powers, the irony of the moment? Their greatest "victories" although tempered with actions and words they, we would surmise, didn't completely understand, took place in gardens. Where man fell and where God was made to anguish and be led away by men, in these green spaces, which were locations not of their choosing,

their final victory (they thought) was also had.

Like Adam, Jesus too was laid to rest in a garden. The Gardener, has, himself, been planted (thus the rebirth of all things). While Adam, in death, went East, Jesus, in death, harrowed the four corners of hell. Again, we see gardens as places of spiritual warfare, cosmic battles, and resistance to the powers. If those powers thought the war was over, the resistance vanquished, we could understand if the setting of a garden was deceptive. What god or power, even if such were cast in flesh, would choose such locations? Instead of grand citadels, estates, manors, castles, pyramids, towers, or great cities, we have dirt, grass, and the cultivation of life, food, and color.

Of course, Mary Magdalene made no mistake. She *had* seen the gardener. All was lost in a garden, and there all was found—there both Adam and Jesus, the Two Men, were laid down and raised up. It all happened in a garden; in fact, one cannot tell the Christian story without referencing gardens. The story of the world, both its violence and redemption, is set in a space of green outline, cultivation, vision, work, and tacit agreement between want, will, desire, and creation. This must have confounded the powers almost as much as the cross. What could we surmise or tease out from this truth? Were the gardens incidental, a mere happenstance? Could the events described have happened anywhere? Perhaps. We must confess it is God who is central in these events and not the setting. Still, I wonder if gardens have a greater significance.

When we think about spiritual warfare and resistance to the powers, we often associate such with prayer and action. This is no doubt true—that both are significant aspects to waging such a war. Let's consider the environment, though, in which we pray and act. If we were to find ourselves in a hostile world, a world in which we were captive, one where we were a minority and without any worldly power, what might our response be? Are there any hints here?

> Build houses and live in them; plant gardens and eat their produce. Take wives and have sons and daughters; take wives for your sons, and give your daughters in marriage, that they may bear sons and daughters; multiply there, and do not decrease. But seek the welfare of the city where I have sent you into exile, and pray to the Lord on its behalf, for in its welfare you will find your welfare. (Jer 29:5–7)

One response, then, is: Life goes on. What does a garden tell us? It tells us that life is to be cultivated. Not death. Every garden is a testament to the proposition that life wins, not death (even if the garden fails—in the very attempt death is reminded of its final end). The preparation, the hoeing, the digging, the weeding, the planting, the tending, are all a testimony. Cultivation, planting, being cognizant of time and season, work, feeling both thorn and profit, all sum up both the curse and the answer. Every garden is both a testament to our fall and our redemption. Gardens, even in our struggles, are sites of hope. We are not sure of the harvest, so many variables are present, and still, we plant. We hope for harvest. We look forward to the bearing of fruit, of life. This very act of hope, this very site requiring such an attitude, is the bane of, and resistance to, the powers.

The very Kingdom of God is compared to planting and gardens. In St. Luke's Gospel (13:19) we are told the Kingdom of God is like a mustard seed a person plants in a garden. Do the powers have anything to fear from this smallest of seeds? Not unless it's planted. Then it eventually becomes a place of rest; a place of gathering. When do the powers tremble? When they see unsanctioned, unofficial, gatherings in places outside the centers of power. However, the idea of something small becoming something large still needs to be understood according to a Kingdom sensibility. Such is noted here by Stanley Hauerwas:

> We must be careful, however, in drawing attention to the 'smallness' of Jesus's beginnings, because such attention can be used to suggest we now know its power in Western Civilization. . . . Accordingly, these parables are not apocalyptically understood, but rather they are interpreted as exemplifications of the modern belief in progress.[2]

It is precisely in the apocalyptic sense that gardens are sites of resistance to the powers. If they try to mimic the progression of village to

---

[2] Stanley Hauerwas, *Brazos Theological Commentary on the Bible, Matthew* (Grand Rapids, Michigan: Brazos Press, 2006), 134.

city, of the idea that larger, or higher, is better, then they are no longer sites of resistance, they are no longer apocalyptic. The movement toward an ever-expanding perimeter of power is related to an understanding of markets, economy, and wealth as a pure reduction—a reduction of everything we see and experience to transaction rather than gift. And we must place the site of gardens within an agrarian, an agricultural circle or framework of viewing creation. Norman Wirzba writes: "Agrarianism tests success and failure not by market share or economic growth but by the health and vitality of a region's entire human and nonhuman neighborhood."[3]

Richard Beck makes these observations: "What strikes me is that, given the military and conquest expectations Israel had for her Messiah, these agricultural metaphors seem very unexpected. When you think of 'kingdom' you don't, I expect, tend to stare at a seed growing, day after day. When you think of 'kingdom' you think of armies, walls, territory, and power. You think of Empire."

Such is exactly the point. The garden is the anti-empire, the counter-kingdom to the kingdoms of this world and their prince. Beck goes on:

And then here comes Jesus with something that sounds like this: "The Kingdom of God is like watching grass grow." How anti-Empire is that vision? And watching the grass grow is a strange sort of Revolution. Watching the grass grow isn't, I'm guessing, anyone's view of The Resistance.

Some other thoughts: What does it mean that the kingdom is sown rather than taken?

What does it mean that the kingdom requires waiting and passivity rather than forcing and activity?

What does it mean that the kingdom begins with the smallest thing rather than the largest?

All that to say, I think there is something deeply subversive going on in Jesus's agricultural parables.[4]

Indeed. The garden operates mysteriously, but still openly—in plain sight. In the rhythms of creation, it speaks to those who will take the time to listen. The powers have no such time. They live in straight lines of speed and chaos, while the garden lives in slower cycles of patient hope as our spherical garden makes its way around the sun. Again, Hauerwas:

There is a kind of madness commensurate with being a disciple of Jesus. To see the world, to understand the kingdom of heaven is like a mustard seed, requires a people who refuse to be hurried. . . . The kingdom of heaven is like a mustard seed . . . because to be drawn into the kingdom of heaven is to participate in God's patience toward his creation.[5]

[3] Norman Wirzba, "Agrarianism after Modernity: An Opening for Grace," in *After Modernity*, ed. James K.A. Smith (Waco, TX: Baylor University Press, 2008), 244.

[4] "The Kingdom as Agriculture," *Experimental Theology*, accessed November 1, 2019.
[5] Stanley Hauerwas, *Brazos Commentary*, *Matthew*, 133.

Churches used to have cemeteries right alongside their own structures. If bored during the sermon, one could ponder the tombstones and markers outside the window. Our earthly end certainly has the power to concentrate the mind. We don't see many cemeteries next to churches anymore, for various reasons. My thought, though, is that what we need are gardens—both of vegetable and flower. A garden on one side, with a cemetery on the other. The garden, among other things, would remind us the cemetery doesn't get the last word. The world encompassed by machinery and the powers are makers of graveyards. The Trinitarian dance, the Wisdom of God, the movement of Spirit, is the cultivation of gardens.

Cities in the biblical narrative seem often to be fists raised in the face of God. Gardens, however, do not aspire to the heavens. What they do aspire to is the redemption of cities. In Revelation 21 and 22 we are shown the beauty of the city coming down, yes, but notice the healing comes from the garden: "The leaves of the tree were for the healing of the nations. No longer will there be anything accursed. . . ." The New Jerusalem becomes the beautiful setting for the healing, for the redemption of the nations, which are known by their grand cities. However, no grand spire, stone, gem, or gold here is healing; rather, it is the leaves—the balm of heaven, the bounty of creation that heals the nations. Only in this way is the city too redeemed. City and garden, like the lion and the lamb, now become friends.

Until then, in the verdant cycles of their spectacular phoenix-like beauty, in living and dying, in the repetition of planting and harvesting, they are the recapitulations, at ground level, revealing, again and again, celestial dramas and eschatological victories. In the simplest and perhaps even crudest of terms: Gardens are the middle-finger to all the principalities, spiritual forces, rulers, and cosmic powers of this present darkness.

The War Against Sloth:
Paul Tyson, Moshe Idel, and the Sleepwalkers

Michael Martin

Paul Tyson, *Seven Brief Lessons on Magic* (Cascade Books, 2019) $13.99;
Moshe Idel, *The Privileged Divine Feminine in the Kabbalah* (Walter de Gruyter, 2019), $114.99

CADEMIA, COUNTER-intuitively perhaps, does not constitute an environment favorable to original thought. This is not necessarily a problem only of our own moment, though it has certainly been exacerbated by the increasing specialization and, at least in the sciences, ungodly sums of money offered in the name of "research." Ideas confronting the status quo are never welcomed with open arms, still less when they're correct. As the great Russian philosopher Nicolai Berdyaev observed in 1943, "The highly cultured man of a certain style usually expresses imitative opinions upon every subject: they are average opinions, *they belong to a group*, though it may well be that this imitativeness belongs to a cultured élite and to a highly select group."[1] Attend any cocktail party of academics for verification.

It is against this backdrop that two recent books—both by academics—offer refreshingly original and innovative explorations at the margins of philosophy and theology. They do so in ways that challenge not only the academic status quo but also the ways non-specialists can think about our ability to understand ourselves and our world and the nature of the Divine.

In *Seven Brief Lesson on Magic*, Australian philosopher Paul Tyson argues that, despite the totalizing effects of secularization, magical belief persists throughout (post)modernity. In the surprisingly short space of sixty-seven pages, Tyson examines (post)modernity's scientism fetish and its (apparent but false) dismissal of magic. He proposes four theories of magic he sees at play: the animist theory, which views Nature as a living being; the Platonist theory, which recognizes how "nature is saturated in transcendent meaning beyond herself"; the supernatural theory, which places the magic beyond Nature; and the anti-magical theory, which *believes* (and "believe" is precisely the

---

[1] Nicolai Berdyaev, *Slavery and Freedom*, trans. R.M. French (New York: Scribner's, 1944), 123. My emphasis.

correct term) that magic does not exist.[2] Tyson digs into each of these proposals to tease out the ways in which human persons and societies have and do actualize these ways of perceiving and acting in the world. As he writes, "To put it bluntly, the primary furnishings of our minds uphold an armed barrier between the way we think about the outer world of factual scientific knowledge and practical technological power and the inner world of imagination, meaning, purpose, and value."[3]

Two important historical events and their cultural aftermath haunt Tyson's little book: the ultimate victory (Pyrrhic, though it be) of *natura pura* during and after the early modern period; and the disenchantment narrative promoted by Max Weber, swallowed (but not digested) by most of those who followed. Also lurking in these *Seven Brief Lessons* are the ideas of Charles Taylor and Peter Harrison, both of whom provide jacket endorsements, as well as William Desmond and John Milbank—all thinkers who have, each in his own way, pushed back against these dominant cultural narratives.

Natura pura ("pure nature") is the proposition that God could withhold his presence from any aspect of Creation, which gave birth to René Descartes's bifurcation of the world into two parts: that which we can discern and exploit (now ostensibly the domain of "science") and that which we cannot, which lies in the supernatural provenance of God. Tyson never mentions it, but Henri de Lubac's seminal study *Surnaturel* (1946)—which has yet to be published in an English translation—informs this part of his argument to a significant degree. The fascinating thing about *natura pura*, a theological proposition, is its role as ground zero for modern science. *Natura pura*, as theological dictum, then, shows precisely how science (or, more properly, *scientism*) is at its foundation a religion. When people say they "believe in science" we need to take that as a faith-based confession as sincere as they come. The only problem is that science has developed a kind of armor or amnesia when it comes to its pedigree. As Tyson writes, "scientific modernity has disavowed its medieval parents, and has constructed its origin myth as a triumphant rebellion against its doddering and oppressive elders."[4]

When it comes to the Weberian disenchantment narrative, Tyson delightfully shows what a two-dimensional piece of pasteboard it is. For Tyson, the disenchantment narrative bears little relationship to our lived experience of the world. In a disenchantment mindset, "values, meaning, and metaphysical orders are—for all scientific and practical purposes—not real features of objective reality. And yet, in our actual human experience, value, meaning, and purpose are fundamental to our ordinary lives. But are these 'secondary' qualities not really real, and is their sense of importance merely a matter of personal or cultural interpretation that has no

[2] Paul Tyson, *Seven Brief Lessons on Magic* (Eugene, OR: Cascade Books, 2019), x.
[3] Ibid., 3.
[4] Ibid., 26.

solid grounding in the way reality is?"[5] As a result, Tyson defines the disenchantment narrative as what it really is: a *mythos*:

> As a *mythos* at one with the supernaturalist and anti-magical metaphysics of scientific modernity, disenchantment is a powerful lifeworld defining myth, ordering our understanding and experience of reality. However, this is in important regards a *false mythology*. For actually, enchantment has not vanished from our ordinary experience of reality. What has really happened is that our understanding of *where* enchantment *is* has moved—under the conditions of scientific modernity—entirely out of the categories of knowledge and factual reality, and completely into the categories of imagination and subjectivity.[6]

For Tyson, then, magic exists precisely in that domain of meaning, purpose, and imagination that science cannot touch but only speculate about (and so unconvincingly). Science may give conveniences to living, but it cannot impart meaning—at least in its various applications, almost all of them tied to some variety of consumerism, capitalism, or control. *Natura pura* dissolves in the face of meaning, leaving science to measurement and the rest to art and religion. Indeed, as did David Bohm before him, Tyson calls science's bluff and lays the blame for many of our challenges on science's very doorstep:

Cataclysmic global climate destabilization combined with billions of insecure people, hawkish "realist" power, and astonishingly destructive military technologies could not only end our life-world, but could wipe humanity from the face of the earth. Science certainly helped us get into this place, but science itself is powerless to help us. It is not the next technological fix that we should pin our hopes for a future on, it is the cultural acquisition of *wisdom* that is our only real hope.[7]

The invocation of Sophia here, I think, is not accidental. For, as Proverbs has it, Sophia rejoices in the habitable part of this earth; and her delights are with the children of men. For these kinds of reasons, Tyson believes "it is entirely reasonable—and indeed, imperative—to see magic as real."[8] For where is Wisdom to be found?

Seven Brief Lesson on Magic is a book geared toward an informed but general reader interested in philosophy, theology, and the history of ideas. Not so with Moshe Idel's *The Privileged Divine Feminine in Kabbalah*,[9] a dense scholarly monograph written for the specialist and highly critical of the commonplaces and scholarly groupthink endemic to academia. It's an inspiration.

Idel's thesis is that the Divine Femi-

---

[5] Ibid., 30–31.
[6] Ibid., 31. Tyson's emphasis.
[7] Ibid., 62. Tyson's emphasis.
[8] Ibid., 67.
[9] Moshe Idel, *The Privileged Divine Feminine in Kabbalah*, Perspectives on Jewish Texts and Contexts 10 (Berlin: Walter de Gruyter, 2019).

nine and its role in Kabbalah has been seriously ignored despite numerous instances of its presence in the kabbalistic literature, especially that from the late medieval period. He bases his claim on three propositions:

> First and most importantly, the elevated ontological status of the Feminine within the theosophical system [within Kabbalah] in comparison to the classical masculine hypostases, *Tiferet* or *Yesod*; second, the dynamic perception of Female in the theosophical realm in comparison to the two main divine masculine powers mentioned above, as She is conceived of as supplying power to other *sefirot*, including the masculine ones; and third, this divine power's ruling over the lower worlds, which is overwhelmingly more conspicuous than the Male's role, despite His being designated as the King and Her being the ultimate aim of the ritual.[10]

Idel's thesis, while radical, is perhaps only incidental to what I take to be his greater project: challenging scholarly groupthink. And in this he pulls no punches. On the first page of the introduction, he explicitly states this: "the ideas addressed below are not in consonance with the rational claims of 'Enlightened' Jews or the all-encompassing vision of an androcentric *imaginaire* put forth in recent decades by scholarly followers of some sort of feminism."[11] Ouch. But he doesn't stop there. Indeed, he has harsh words for both the purveyors of

a "phallocentric" interpretation of Kabbalah as well as those marketing a facile "feminist" approach. The former he accuses of neglecting or suppressing what to him is patently obvious in Kabbalah.[12] Of the latter he laments: "What could have been a fresh approach to Kabbalah, in this case, some fresh questions adopted from feminist theories, has turned into an axiom, actually an academic ahistorical dogma, allowing no exceptions, and speaking openly, and amusingly I must say, about detractors, heresies and obsessions, in publications that are deemed academic."[13]

Idel's method is more in resonance with what I have called elsewhere an "agapeic criticism."[14] His approach resides in a porosity in presence to the texts before him:

> Scholars who try to subsume medieval traditions to fashionable but unsuitable modern theories merely obscure texts by inventing harmonizing interpretations. I propose more flexible approaches: a toolbox of methods, in fact, will facilitate a proper understanding of modes of thought on sex and gender that differ so dramatically from the modern ones. As part of a polychromatic approach to this literature, scholarship should pay greater attention to the expressions of ambivalence toward the Female. Moreover, modesty and

---

10 Ibid., 12.
11 Ibid., 1.

12 Ibid., 198.
13 Ibid., 206.
14 Michael Martin, "Criticism and Contemplation" in *The Incarnation of the Poetic Word: Theological Essays on Poetry and Philosophy / Philosophical Essays on Poetry and Theology* (Kettering, OH: Angelico Press, 2017).

less aggressive language may also serve as indispensable qualities for sensitive reading of the texts and then interpreting them. By listening only to one melody, scholars are prone to be deaf to other important voices.[15]

So much for his method, which is much to be recommended.

Idel's investigation begins with a simple proposition attributed to Aristotle: "The first in thought is last in action." Applying this to theosophical Kabbalah, and in particular to the kabbalistic Tree of Life, Idel argues that not only is the Divine Feminine the *telos* of Kabbalah (and by implication Creation), but is also its source; or, spoken in the idiom of the Tree of Life, *Keter* as well as *Malkhut*. As he explains, "The view of the divine Feminine as recipient is connected to Her being the Ruler, namely of allocating power, and the understanding of Her nature solely as recipient would be a distortion."[16] He locates this notion all through the literature, in Moses Cordovero and Isaac Luria to cite the most familiar, and his discoveries bear an unmistakable sophiological imprint. In his discussion of Luria, for example, he touches on language evocative of Revelation 21:

> The preeminence of the Female, *Malkhut*, is evident, both in the primordial past and in the eschatological future, when She is depicted as even transcending the light of the Sun, namely the Male, as Her Husband. Her description

in the eschaton as higher than the sun is indicative of the *imaginaire* of Her grandeur.[17]

What is radical in Idel's reading of these texts, then, is not that he brings a profoundly idiosyncratic and politically subjective lens to his examination, but that he *actually reads what is there, as it is.* That such an approach could ever be considered controversial speaks to how compromised the academic project is by ideas superfluous and ephemeral, even if dangerous. In fact, one could argue that the superfluous and ephemeral nature of academic discourse is the root and branch of its estrangement from the supposedly scholarly ethos of truth-seeking. In his dedication to unveiling the truth of his subject, Idel proves himself an almost solitary beacon in the darkworld of academia.

Both of these books, each with its various commitments and intended audiences, offer signs of hope. Tyson's *Seven Brief Lessons on Magic* is an ideal text for, among other things, providing undergraduates with an alternative epistemology from the totalizing and banal scientism many of them bring with them to college (I have used it for a course on the history of thought). At a cultural moment when scientism has been vying for absolute hegemony, his book could not have arrived soon enough. Idel's *The Privileged Divine Feminine in Kabbalah,* on the other hand, opens a path for scholars not only of religion and philosophy but for any discipline, a path toward integrity and clear-sightedness uncom-

---

[15] Idel, 200.
[16] Ibid., 38.

[17] Ibid., 107.

promised by the excrescences of politics and turf wars.

Finally, these two books participate in a Sophiology that is attentive to the World as It Is, to Things as They Are. Tyson does so implicitly in his method, which, true to his own preference for the Platonist Theory of Magic, avows that "nature is saturated in transcendent meaning beyond herself." Idel's latent Sophiology, or at least that of the subjects under his consideration, clearly, is more explicit as it points to a sophiological eschaton hidden since the foundation of the world.

THE SIGNATURE OF ALL THINGS

Kenneth Rexroth

I.

My head and shoulders, and my book
In the cool shade, and my body
Stretched bathing in the sun, I lie
Reading beside the waterfall –
Boehme's *Signature of All Things.*
Through the deep July day the leaves
Of the laurel, all the colors
Of gold, spin down through the moving
Deep laurel shade all day. They float
On the mirrored sky and forest
For a while, and then, still slowly
Spinning, sink through the crystal deep
Of the pool to its leaf gold floor.
The saint saw the world as streaming
In the electrolysis of love.
I put him by and gaze through shade
Folded into shade of slender
Laurel trunks and leaves filled with sun.
The wren broods in her moss domed nest.
A newt struggles with a white moth
Drowning in the pool. The hawks scream,
Playing together on the ceiling
Of heaven. The long hours go by.
I think of those who have loved me,
Of all the mountains I have climbed,
Of all the seas I have swum in.
The evil of the world sinks.
My own sin and trouble fall away
Like Christian's bundle, and I watch
My forty summers fall like falling
Leaves and falling water held
Eternally in summer air.

II.

Deer are stamping in the glades,
Under the full July moon.
There is a smell of dry grass
In the air, and more faintly,
The scent of a far off skunk.
As I stand at the wood's edge,
Watching the darkness, listening
To the stillness, a small owl
Comes to the branch above me,
On wings more still than my breath.
When I turn my light on him,
His eyes glow like drops of iron,
And he perks his head at me,
Like a curious kitten.
The meadow is bright as snow.
My dog prows the grass, a dark
Blur in the blur of brightness
I walk to the oak grove where
The Indian village was once.
There, in blotched and cobwebbed light
And dark, dim in the blue haze,
Are twenty Holstein heifers,
Black and white, all lying down,
Quietly together, under
The huge trees rooted in the graves.

III.
When I dragged the rotten log
From the bottom of the pool,
It seemed heavy as stone.
I let it lie in the sun
For a month; and then chopped it
Into sections, and split them
For kindling, and spread them out
To dry some more. Late that night;
After reading for hours,
While moths rattled at the lamp,
The saints and the philosophers
On the destiny of man;
I went out on my cabin porch,
And looked up through the black forest
At the swaying islands of stars.
Suddenly I saw at my feet,
Spread on the floor of night, ingots
Of quivering phosphorescence,
And all about were scattered chips
Of pale cold light that was alive.

Contributors

Ruth Asch has poetry and stories buried deep under the preoccupations of a job at a mental health clinic and mothering five characterful kids. She has one book, *Reflections*, and many poems and stories in journals and anthologies real and virtual.

Isak Bond is a husband, father, actor, high school poetry teacher and drama coach from Phoenix, Arizona. His work has appeared in *Spilled Milk Magazine, Four Chambers, Convivium, rinky dink press, Presence,* and previously in *Jesus the Imagination.* He likes Shakespeare and Joyce. Most recently, he directed a high school production of *Oedipus the Tyrant.* When he is not teaching or acting, you can catch him and his typewriter on the street writing poetry for strangers, some of which he posts on Instagram as @giddyface.

Cheri Davis is a photographer/visual artist and musician from Philadelphia. She feels most at home among the mystics she reads about.

Tyler DeLong currently works as an outdoor and woodworking educator for adolescents and families who have experienced trauma. Tyler and his family have a small homestead and workshop in the village of Mechanicsburg in rural Ohio.

Jon Egan is a musician and writer based in Liverpool, England and was a founding member of the music collective, Revolutionary Army of the Infant Jesus. He is an associate with the post-Liberal think tank, ResPublica and is an Orthodox Christian.

Jonathan Monroe Geltner has translated Paul Claudel's *Five Great Odes,* now available from Angelico Press, and his novel *Absolute Music* is forthcoming from Slant. He lives in Ann Arbor, Michigan with his wife and two sons.

Katie Hartsock is the author of the poetry collection *Bed of Impatiens* (Able Muse Press, 2016). She teaches at Oakland University in Michigan, where she lives with her husband and sons.

Paul Hunter is a native of New York, but now lives with his wife and two children (who would like to live entirely on berries) in Beaufort, SC. He is an Episcopal priest and teaches Latin at Holy Trinity Classical Christian School.

Andrew Kuiper lives in Hillsdale, Michigan with his wife and three children. He has been published in *The Regensburg Forum, Touchstone Magazine, The Imaginative Conservative, Church Life Journal,* and *The Lamp.* He is the main contributor to the online theological blog at publishing company *Ex Fontibus* and co-editor of a volume of Nicholas of Cusa translations (forthcoming Notre Dame University Press).

Darrell Lackey is a graduate of the University of San Francisco and Golden Gate Baptist Theological Seminary. He and his wife reside in Northern California. Darrell's other writings can be found at: https://www.patreon.com/DarrellL?fan_landing=true.

Michael Martin is the editor of *Jesus the Imagination*.

Scot F. Martin teaches high school English in SE Michigan as well as co-sponsoring his school's ecology club. He lives near a river, but dreams of life with a bigger yard in another watershed with his wife, two children, and two cats.

Philippa Martyr is an academic, researcher, writer, and student. She lives in Perth, Western Australia.

Jeremy Naydler is a philosopher and gardener, and author of several books including *In the Shadow of the Machine* (2018), *Gardening as a Sacred Art* (2011) and a book of poems, *Soul Gardening* (2006). His essay is based on an illustrated talk given in the greenhouse at Worton Organic Garden, in Oxfordshire, on a magical evening in October 2018, as a contribution to the Oxford Chamber Music Festival, in which the poems were recited to the accompaniment of tanpura, voice, and drum played by Felix Padel. The essay was first published by Abzu Press in 2018. All the poems are by Jeremy Naydler. "To the Gentle Worm" was previously published in

Soul Gardening (Oxford: Godstow Press, 2006); "Praise" was previously published in *The Bridge* (Oxford: Abzu Press, 2000).

Kenneth Rexroth (1905–1982) was a poet, translator, and literary critic and one of the central figures of the San Francisco Renaissance.

John R. P. Russell is a husband, a father of four, and a priest for the Byzantine Ruthenian Catholic Eparchy of Parma. He is the administrator of St. Stephen Byzantine Catholic Church in Allen Park, Michigan, a lifelong artist, and an occasional poet.

Harpist, singer, composer, educator, and clinician **Therese Schroeder-Sheker** has maintained dual careers in classical music and end-of-life care. She founded the palliative medical modality of music-thanatology and its flagship organization The Chalice of Repose Project. Therese made her Carnegie Hall debut in 1980, recorded for American and European labels, and publishes frequently on contemplative musicianship, music in medicine, and the women mystics.

Tom Sturch is a husband to his favorite reader and father to adult sons. He lives in Tampa, Florida and keeps a small landscape architecture practice. About eight years ago he discovered poetry (or perhaps the other way around) as another way to enjoy place-making and way-finding. His messy garden provides endless inspiration. Works of Tom's have been published in *St. Katherine Review*, *Gargoyle*, *Relief Journal*, and *Jesus the Imagination*.

R. Bratten Weiss is a freelance academic and organic grower residing in rural Ohio. Her creative work has appeared in a number of publications, including a collaborative chapbook, *Mud Woman*, with Joanna Penn Cooper (Dancing Girl Press, 2018). Her chapbook *Talking to Snakes* is forthcoming from Ethel in spring 2020.

Rick Yoder is pursuing a Ph.D. in History at Pennsylvania State University, where he specializes in Jansenism, mysticism, and gender in early modern France. His poetry has appeared in *Jesus The Imagination*, *ASH*, and *The Emma Press Anthology of Contemporary Gothic Verse* (2019), while his prose has appeared in *The Church Times* (UK), *First Things*, and *Church Life Journal*. He blogs regularly at *The Amish Catholic*.

Made in the USA
Coppell, TX
26 September 2020